TEACHING ADULTS
HOW TO SWIM

Unlock The Art Of Adult Instruction
And Overcome The Challenges Of
Adult Swimming Lessons

A Swimming Teacher's Guide

Mark Young

Teaching Adults How To Swim

A Catalogue record for this book is available from the British Library
ISBN 978-0-9954842-9-0

Published by: Educate & Learn Publishing, Hertfordshire, UK

Illustrations and diagrams by Mark Young, courtesy of Poser V6.0

Design and typeset by Mark Young

Photographs courtesy of depositphotos.com and Mark Young
Front cover image courtesy of depositphotos.com, stock image id 248927310

Note: This book is intended for guidance and support only. The material contained here should accompany additional course material set on an official swimming teaching course by an official Swimming Association. Neither the author nor the publisher can accept responsibility for any injury or loss sustained as a result of the use of this material.

Author Online!

For more resources and swimming help visit Mark Young's website at

www.swim-teach.com

Mark Young is a well-established swimming instructor with decades of experience teaching thousands of adults and children to swim. He has taken scared children and adults who fear water and made them happy and confident swimmers. He has also turned many of average ability into advanced swimmers. This book draws on his experiences and countless successes to bring together this informative and detailed guide to becoming a successful swimming teacher and teaching outstanding swimming lessons.

Also by Mark Young

Teaching Guides
How To Be A Swimming Teacher
101 Swimming Lesson Plans For Swimming Teachers
How To Teach Front Crawl
How To Teach Breaststroke
How To Teach Backstroke
How To Teach Butterfly

Learn to Swim Guides
The Complete Beginners Guide to Swimming
How To Swim Front Crawl
How To Swim Breaststroke
How To Swim Backstroke
How To Swim Butterfly
The Swimming Strokes Book
Teach Your Child To Swim

An electronic version of this book is available from Swim-Teach.com

Contents

Page

Introduction

Everyone who arrives at the poolside ready to learn how to swim is different, and adults are no exception. However, adult swimming lessons need a different approach than swimming lessons for children. Swimming teachers must adapt their lessons to help accommodate adult learners and their individual needs.

Barriers, Obstacles and Challenges

Barriers, Obstacles and Challenges

Adults face many barriers and have several obstacles to overcome when faced with the challenge of learning how to swim. The five most common obstacles are:

- Fear or Anxiety Related to Water
- Perceived Vulnerability or Feeling Embarrassed
- Physical Fitness or Health Issues
- Lack of Available Resources
- Time Constraints

Fear or Anxiety Related to Water

For many adults, fear of water or underlying anxieties can be significant barriers to learning to swim. This psychological challenge can stem from past experiences (like near-drowning incidents), watching or hearing stories of water incidents, or simply from a fear of the unknown.

An example might be an adult who had a scary childhood experience around water, where they accidentally fell in and struggled. Such challenges are difficult to overcome because they are deeply rooted in an individual's personal experiences and emotions, which can take significant time and patience to address.

It is possible to overcome this fear with the help and support of a good swimming teacher. The approach here is to take it slow, build confidence, and help them conquer their fear in a comfortable and supportive environment.

All swimming teachers understand that the fear of water can be a significant obstacle for adults wanting to learn how to swim. Always treat your pupils as individuals and design your lessons to help them gradually become familiar with water and build confidence. Start them in the pool's shallow end with simple confidence-building exercises and move on only when they feel ready.

Perceived Vulnerability or Feeling Embarrassed

This challenge involves feeling exposed or vulnerable in a swimsuit or swimming attire, often related to body image or self-consciousness. It's a common sticking point because swimming requires wearing clothing that may feel revealing, making some adults uncomfortable or insecure. Picture a person who avoids swimming lessons because they feel self-conscious about their body in a swimsuit. Overcoming this challenge can be difficult due to personal insecurities about appearance. It often requires a substantial boost of self-esteem and acceptance of one's body image.

Some adults feel they should've learned to swim as children and, as a result, feel embarrassed at the prospect of learning to swim later in life.

Remind your pupils that, whilst every adult in the class has insecurities, they are not alone in this journey; everyone is there to support each other. They are all in the same boat! Let them know:
'You have made the bold step of coming to the pool today to learn how to swim. Hundreds of adults sat at home, wishing they could do the same. Be proud of yourself.'

Physical Fitness or Health Issues

Because swimming is a physical activity that requires strength, flexibility, and endurance, certain diseases or health issues, like arthritis, obesity, heart conditions, etc., can cause an adult considering swimming lessons to think twice.

For example, an overweight man might feel considerable strain in his joints during swimming, or an individual with respiratory issues may struggle with breath control.

These challenges are often difficult to overcome as they involve personal health and physical capacity, which require medical consultations, physical therapy, or long-term fitness work to alleviate.

It is important to get the point across to your pupils that one key reason to learn to swim is the numerous health benefits. Swimming is a low-impact yet highly effective form of exercise that can boost cardiovascular health, improve strength and flexibility, and help manage weight.

Attending swimming lessons and learning to swim is an ideal workout option for all ages, including older adults.

Learning to swim as an adult also provides mental health benefits. Overcoming fears and achieving new skills can boost self-esteem and confidence. Swimming has also proven to reduce stress and promote relaxation, offering a valuable outlet for managing daily pressures.

Swimming is a low-impact exercise often recommended for people with various health conditions, as it puts less strain on joints than other forms of exercise. As a swimming teacher, it is essential that you tailor your swimming lessons to suit the fitness level and health condition of your pupils. Learning to swim is a physical activity by its very nature, and the strength and endurance of your pupils will gradually improve by default. You must, however, monitor them closely as they learn and ensure they are working safely. Ensure they are being appropriately-exerted, and regularly check in with them by asking them how they feel.

If they have any existing medical conditions, adults should seek medical advice before starting any new exercise program, including swimming lessons. Their doctor or physician will very likely recommend they take up swimming lessons.

Lack of Available Resources

Some adults might need help finding appropriate resources, such as swimming pools, coaches, or adult swimming classes. The lack of resources can be a significant obstacle because immersion, regular practice, and professional instruction are crucial for learning swimming. An example might be an individual living in a geographically isolated area with limited access to swimming pools or instructors. This challenge is difficult to overcome due to location, transportation, finances, or the availability of suitable infrastructure and services.

Time Constraints

Adult life is often filled with responsibilities and obligations, such as work, family, and social commitments, which may leave little time for swimming lessons. This is typically an obstacle because swimming, like any skill, requires a dedicated and consistent time commitment to learn and practice. For instance, a busy working mother or a businessman with a hectic schedule might find it challenging to fit swimming lessons into their daily lives. Overcoming this challenge requires careful planning, time management, and, often, the ability to make swimming a priority. That's why it's tough for many adults to overcome.

Time is precious, especially for busy adults. To accommodate their busy schedules, you can offer flexible scheduling options, including early morning and late evening classes, if your arrangements allow for that. You could provide intensive lessons over a few days or a weekend. Even a small amount of consistent, regular practice is better than none.

Adults vs Children

Adults vs Children

Why Is Teaching Adults To Swim Different To Teaching Children?

Physical Differences

Adults have different physical attributes compared to children, including height, weight, muscle mass, and coordination, which influence the way they learn to swim. Adult learners often require time to get used to the water and may need different types and amounts of flotation devices during initial lessons.

Cognitive Differences

Children learn best through play and exploration, but adults typically prefer a structured, goal-oriented approach. So, swimming teachers must tailor their lessons accordingly. For example, a child's swimming lesson might involve games and fun activities, whereas an adult lesson might focus more on a specific technique or exercise.

Language and Communication

Adults usually require more detailed explanations about the mechanics of swimming strokes. The language, phrases, and communication strategies you use when teaching will differ significantly. For instance, children might respond better to imaginative language, like "pretend you're a dolphin." At the same time, adults might prefer more technical language, such as "extend your arm fully and rotate your shoulder."

Previous Experience and Fear

Adults often bring past experiences and fears with them to their swimming lessons. Some may have had a traumatic experience in the water or have developed a fear over time. With these adults, you will need to spend more time helping them to overcome these barriers, using strategies such as gradual exposure and positive reinforcement.

Learning Pace

Adults often take longer to learn new skills than children, who are still developing their motor skills and can adapt and learn faster. Therefore, adult swimming lessons may need to progress at a slower pace, with more repetition and practice.

Time Commitment

Adults usually have busier schedules than children, juggling work and family commitments. Time constraints like these may mean they cannot attend lessons as regularly or practice as often.

Motivation

Children are often enrolled in swimming lessons by their parents and may be motivated by fun. Conversely, adults are generally self-motivated and have specific goals, such as fitness, a vacation or having fun with their children or grandchildren. Understanding these motivations can help tailor the lessons and keep the learners engaged.

Feedback

Adults often expect immediate, detailed feedback and are more self-critical than children. Be prepared to provide constructive criticism and encouragement to help your adult pupils improve their technique and confidence.

Risk of Injury

Adults are more likely to suffer from health problems or physical limitations that could lead to injury in the pool. Therefore, as a swimming teacher, you must be aware of these potential issues and adapt your teaching methods as required.

Social Aspect

Adults may view swimming lessons as a social activity and enjoy interacting with their peers. Incorporating paired exercises or group activities can add an enjoyable social element to the sessions.

Teaching Qualities

Teaching Qualities

What makes a good swimming teacher for adults?

A good swimming teacher requires a wide range of qualities. You will probably be better in some areas than others, but as you gain experience, you will build your competence in all areas.

To be a good teacher and role model to your pupils, you must possess some essential qualities.

Knowledge

A sound understanding of your subject gains respect from pupils, and your adult pupils will gain confidence in you from it. You will need to keep your knowledge up to date and always admit when you don't know the answer, but make it your business to find out!

Empathy

Teaching swimming requires empathy on all levels. An adult who fears water or is embarrassed needs your understanding and support. Adult progress is notoriously slow, so empathy is just one quality you will need to help ease this pressure.

Patience

All of the above examples that require empathy will also test your patience. As a swimming teacher teaching adults, you must accept that progress will be slow. No one will be more frustrated than your pupils, so extending your patience and control will help support and encourage them in the way they need.

Effective Communication

As a teacher, your job is to pass on information effectively and clearly. Your ability to do this will determine how quickly your pupils learn. Knowledge of your subject is also essential, but conveying that knowledge is far more critical. You could be a world expert on the human body and the scientific principles behind swimming. Still, you are not a good teacher if you cannot pass that expertise on to eager-to-learn pupils clearly and concisely!

Basic Principles of Effective Communication

Positioning

The teacher's placement on the poolside in front of the class is crucial for effective communication. Every pupil in the class must be able to see and hear the teacher at all times, and the teacher must have easy sight of all pupils in the water.

Clarity

Passing information on clearly will ensure your pupils can follow your instructions and carry them out effectively and in the way you intended.

Conciseness

Keep your teaching concise to ensure your pupils understand and absorb the correct information. Although adults can listen and absorb longer and more detailed instructions than children, they still need each instruction to be concise and to the point.

Accuracy

Your teaching must be accurate, as your adult pupils will remember and repeat it. Inaccuracy will result in them not learning and their progress being even slower, which will, in turn, damage your reputation.

Enthusiasm

A sure way to motivate your class and get results is to have an enthusiastic approach. Enthusiasm is infectious, and if you are full of it when you teach, your pupils will put every effort into what you ask them to do.

Appropriateness

The teaching points and practices you use will determine the success and outcome of the lesson. If your methods are inappropriate, the pupils will not learn, and the lesson will become pointless.

Two-way

Communication works both ways. Ask your pupils questions and listen carefully to those who answer and how they answer. Encourage them to give feedback on an exercise they have attempted, especially if you see that they were less successful than you or they had hoped.

Motivation

As a teacher, you are also a motivator. Some pupils you teach will need more motivation than others. Most adults have a desire to learn to swim, and that alone is their motivation. However, you will find some adults lacking in motivation, which could be due to their slow progress or a less-than-successful lesson the previous week. Either way, a motivating teacher brings out the best in pupils.

Praise

Praise is the easiest and most common form of motivation. Remember to praise effort as well as success.

As a swimming teacher, you should praise and encourage pupils throughout your lessons. Thumbs up, high fives and clapping are ways to give continuous praise during the lesson. Combine these with phrases like "That's brilliant, well done, keep going, you're doing well," and they will enhance your pupils' sense of achievement. It will help them feel good, which will help with their learning and progression.

Feedback

Feedback is a more detailed, constructive form of praise. It gives the pupils a clearer picture of their performance and progress. If feedback is to be motivational, it has to be positive.

For example, a swimmer unsuccessfully returns to the poolside after practising front crawl leg kick. Your job is to teach and motivate them. Your feedback should go something like this:

'*Well done, that was a good try*' (praise for the effort)
'*You were pointing your toes, which is good. Well done.*' (positive feedback)

'*Try again, and kick your legs from your hips this time.*' (feedback in the form of a teaching point)

Avoid negative feedback, for example, 'Don't *bend your legs.*'

Goal setting

Goal setting is an ideal way of motivating pupils. Setting a realistic and appropriate goal will encourage progress, and goals come in many forms. Badges and awards are the most common and popular types of goals, but they are more appropriate for children. Setting goals for adults can be swimming a short distance, such as 5 or 10 metres, gliding from the poolside and standing up unaided, or it could be as simple as attending lessons each week for a set number of weeks. Human nature dictates that we are motivated by our perception of our ability. Therefore, it is vitally important that all goals set be measurable and achievable in a realistic time scale.

Adapting Your Teaching Style

Adapting Your Teaching Style

When teaching adults to swim, it is crucial to adapt your teaching style to suit them. Adults will arrive at the poolside in all shapes and sizes and with different confidence levels. However, one thing they will all have in common is that they will all appreciate a relaxed and informal approach to learning to swim.

Slow progress is normal when teaching adults to swim and should not be viewed negatively. Most adults require a more detailed explanation when giving instructions and teaching points. For example, they will want to know why they need to kick their legs a certain way.

As a swimming teacher, here are a few things you can do:

- Be calm, relaxed and informal in your teaching style. This approach will help to relax your adult and keep them at ease.
- Adjust your expectations accordingly.
- Take their limitations into account when planning. Exercises and drills that suit one swimmer may not work for another.
- Be flexible in your approach. For example, fins or hand paddles (usually used in advanced drills) can benefit adult beginners so long as they do not become reliant on them.
- Be sensitive to their frustrations, and always be supportive and empathetic in your response.
- Above all, use plenty of praise to stimulate and maintain motivation. At the end of each lesson, pick out the parts in which they showed progress and highlight them as achievements of the session, however small they may be.

Although the learning process for adults may vary from that of kids, adults usually have a better understanding of mechanics and body movements, which can benefit their learning. Also, adults can communicate their fears and concerns more effectively, enabling you as their swimming instructor to tailor the lessons to their specific needs.

Teaching adults to swim requires patience, perseverance, and a personal approach. Many adults fear water due to traumatic experiences, but overcoming this fear is entirely possible. As a good instructor, you will know how to take it slow, build their confidence, and provide them with a comfortable and supportive environment in which they can conquer their fears.

Different Abilities

Teaching adults to swim can be more challenging and complex than teaching children. However, it can also be more rewarding, particularly when you have helped adult learners overcome their fears and gain confidence in the water.

The Non-Swimmer

Non-swimmers arrive on the poolside from all age groups and walks of life. Some will come with built-in courage and confidence, while others will be nervous and anxious. Whatever 'non-swimmers' attend your swimming lessons, treat them equally by starting at the very beginning and teaching them everything!

Non-swimmers may lack confidence in the water and be fearful in a swimming pool, especially initially.

The learning outcomes for the non-swimmer should include:
- being able to confidently and safely enter the exit the water
- gaining confidence by moving (walking) around in the water
- being able to regain a standing position in the water from a prone position
- being able to submerge under the water
- to show progression towards floating independently (either stationary or while moving in the water)

Beginner Swimmers

Beginner swimmers can independently get around in the water but would not be safe out of their depth without buoyancy aids or assistance. They may be able to swim short distances but need more style or technique.

The learning outcomes for the beginner swimmer should include:
- being able to propel themselves through the water on the front and back (with buoyancy aids)
- beginning to show basic stroke techniques
- beginning to show a streamlined body position from a push and glide

- being able to swim about ten metres without putting their feet down in both the prone and supine body positions

Intermediate Swimmers

Intermediate swimmers can confidently swim 10 metres or more on their front and back.

The learning outcomes for Intermediate swimmers should include:
- strokes improvement that shows good streamlining
- front crawl, back crawl, and breaststroke are recognisable strokes
- to develop controlled breathing techniques relevant to each swimming stroke
- develop the timing of the strokes as competence increases
- maintain stroke technique over longer distances of continuous swimming

Advanced Swimmers

These swimmers should be capable of sustaining a good stroke over increasing distances.

The learning outcomes for advanced swimmers should include:
- being able to swim front crawl, back crawl and breaststroke with smooth, fluid movements
- to develop and improve butterfly stroke

- to create increased efficiency by maintaining streamlined movements over longer distances
- to keep an efficient pace and stroke rate over longer distances
- to develop accurate breath control through increased strength and stamina

Equipment

Floats and kickboards

When used correctly, swimming floats can help develop specific parts of a swimming stroke. They are suitable for non-swimmers up to advanced swimmers and ideal for teaching adults.

Swimming teachers use swim floats in lessons for many different exercises. Non-swimmers can use them to strengthen parts of their swimming strokes, and established swimmers can use them to isolate and perfect technique.

For example, the weak non-swimmer can use two floats, one placed under each arm, to help strengthen their leg kick. The floats will provide stability and help boost confidence whilst encouraging a fast and furious leg kick.

Advantages:

- Very versatile and can help enhance a wide range of swimming exercises.
- Can be used in addition to other buoyancy aids.
- Can be used in place of other types of swimming aids to encourage progression and enhance strength and stamina.
- When used individually, floats can help gain leg or arm strength.
- Fine-tune technique by encouraging a swimmer to focus on a particular area of their swimming stroke.
- Cheap to buy and easy to store. Also easy to use with large groups.

Disadvantages:

- Require close supervision with non-swimmers.

Common Mistakes To Watch Out For

Misusing a float is difficult because they are such a simple piece of swimming equipment. However, there are a couple of points to watch out for when using floats to teach adults.

Firstly, it is common for adults to grip the float too tightly, especially if they are nervous beginners. They squeeze the float in their hand, resulting in a very tired hand grip and a focus away from the part of their swimming they are supposed to concentrate on.

Secondly, it is common for adults to bear their weight onto the float without knowing they are doing so, causing it to submerge. Once again, this is easily done by the nervous beginner as they attempt to rise above the water surface instead of lying on the surface. Reassuring and helping them relax by advising them to "let the float support you" will go some way to helping pupils get the most out of swimming floats.

These common problems can take time to fix as the swimmer learns to relax and become comfortable in the water. As long as you, the teacher, are aware and the swimmer is made aware, your adults can gradually progress.

Woggle or Noodle

One of the most popular buoyancy aids, the swimming noodle, is a simple polythene foam cylinder—one of the most popular and widely used floats during swimming lessons.

Sometimes called a 'woggle', it is cheap to make and buy and easy to use with large group swimming lessons.

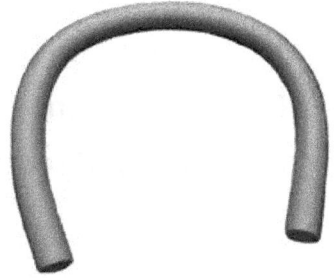

The main advantage is that it provides good support while allowing the swimmer to move their arms and legs. Thus, the swimmer can learn and experience propulsion from both arms and legs through the water.

The noodle is very versatile. Adults can easily add and remove it as it is not a fixed aid, and it is perfect for adult beginners learning breaststroke technique.

Advantages:

- Provides a good level of support for adults of all sizes.
- Gives a sense of independence in the water with the minimum of support.
- Allows freedom of movement.
- Boosts confidence in the nervous beginner.
- Easy to fit and remove, so it is ideal for group swimming lessons.

Disadvantages:

- Limited or no use for advanced swimmers.
- Nervous swimmers can 'clamp' it between their body and their arms, restricting their arm action.

Fins

For adults learning to swim, swimming fins are a great way to help develop a correct kicking action for front crawl and backstroke. They help keep the feet and toes in a pointed position and encourage the ankle and knee joints to relax during the kicking action.

However, swimmers and teachers must not become overly reliant on fins. They are useful for helping to build strength and power, but swimmers should be encouraged to take them off and try to transpose the feeling into their feet by making their feet behave like fins as they swim.

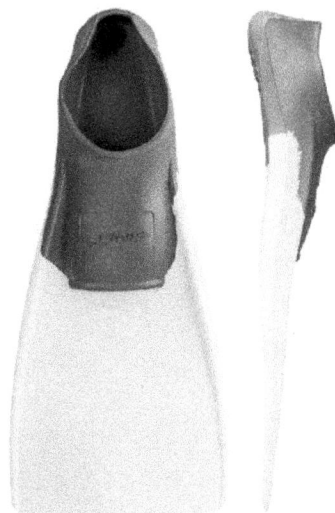

Teach The Important Basics First

Teach The Important Basics First

During the initial stages of teaching adults to swim, swimming teachers must introduce some essential basics. These vital swimming basics include:

- entering the water
- movement through the water
- getting the face wet
- breathing
- submerging
- floating
- standing up from face down and face up positions
- gliding

Teaching these basics as early as possible builds and enhances confidence in the water and provides a solid foundation for adults to learn the four basic swimming strokes.

Water Confidence

Some pupils quickly become confident in water, but others may take much longer. It may take an adult pupil longer to become confident and feel relaxed in the water than a younger pupil.

Causes of fear for new pupils include:

- the sheer vastness of the water alone can be intimidating
- the instability felt when walking in water
- the fear of water getting into the eyes
- the fear of lifting the feet off the pool floor
- the lack of ability to regain the standing position if the feet are lifted off the floor
- the fear of sinking
- the inability to breathe

Overcoming Fear

As a swimming teacher, it is vitally important to show understanding and empathy towards pupils who display feelings of fear or anxiety. Their fears will be the root cause of many of the problems you must overcome together.

Pupils who are scared or fearful should be allowed to progress at *their* own pace. As their teacher, you should ensure they are fully confident before moving on to the next exercise rather than being pushed along to speed up progress. Forcing a pupil to try an exercise when frightened can indefinitely put them off swimming. You should also ensure that the more confident pupils do not intimidate the less confident ones by splashing or being inappropriately over-enthusiastic.

Entering the Water

For adult non-swimmers, entering the water can be hugely daunting. Pupils must do it safely and appropriately. Teach your pupils to use the following entries accordingly:

Stepping in using the poolside steps

Entering via the pool's steps is the best entry for the nervous non-swimmer. Pupils should be encouraged to hold on to the rails with both hands and step down one step at a time.

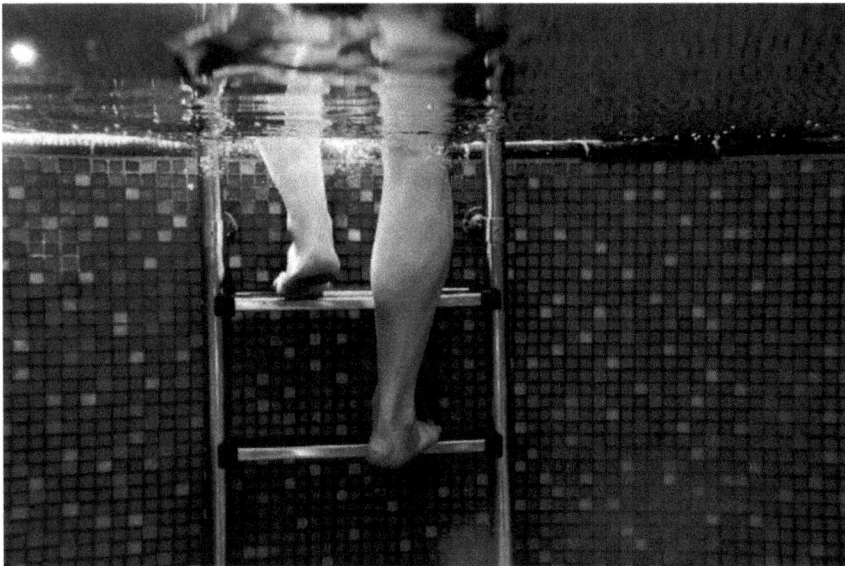

This safe and gradual entry allows the pupil to take their time. However, this method is very time-consuming for larger groups.

The sitting swivel entry

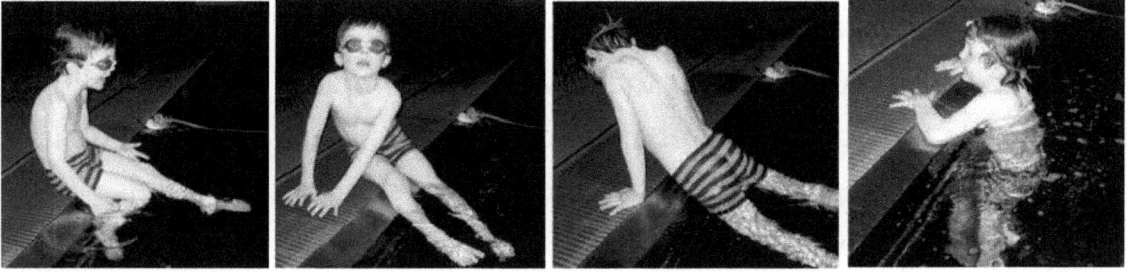

This entry is the safest and quickest for larger groups and works best on deck-level swimming pools. From a sitting position, with legs in the water, you should instruct the pupils to place both hands to one side and turn their backs to the water. They should then lower themselves gradually into the water, keeping hold of the poolside.

Jumping Entry

Before jumping, the teacher should consider the water's depth compared to the pupils' size before using a jumping entry. You should then instruct your pupils to start with their toes over the edge of the poolside, jump away from the poolside, and bend their knees on landing. This entry is best for more confident pupils, who should always be in water of a depth they can stand up.

Movement Through the Water

During the early stages of learning to swim, pupils must get used to the water slowly, gradually, and at their own pace. Simple walking or sliding movements through the water are excellent confidence builders. Pupils should be encouraged to move around using their arms and hands whilst walking to get a 'feel' for the water.

Some adults may require floats or buoyancy aids to support them while moving through the water. This is more common in nervous beginners. Buoyancy aids should be discouraged as soon as confidence builds before pupils become dependent.

Movement patterns can take the form of shapes made on the pool floor with the feet, changes of direction, and collecting a floating object such as a ball. As confidence builds further, pupils can hop, skip and jump.

Breathing

When moving through the water, the ability to breathe can be a fear that holds back pupils. As a swimming teacher, you want your pupils to grow in confidence and become competent swimmers. Therefore, they need to be able to breathe out in the water, control their breathing and be confident with water around their face, mouth, and nose.

Breathing is an involuntary action that happens automatically; therefore, most pupils have never considered it. When in the water, breathing is a conscious, physical act, which, for some, can be a cause of great stress

Pupils who are new or nervous about swimming can become distressed or anxious about putting their face in the water and learning to breathe. Therefore, as a swimming teacher, you must develop breathing practices at the pupils' own pace.

Teaching practices:
- cupping water in the hands and then wetting the face
- blowing bubbles across the water surface
- partially submerging the face to mouth or nose level
- submerging the body under the water to collect an object that has been partially or fully submerged

Underwater Confidence

The ability to submerge the face is arguably one of the most critical stages of learning to swim. Some adult beginners arrive with this ability and only need to know how to breathe whilst swimming. For others, it will be a terrifying task. You will need to use a gentle and gradual approach for these pupils. You proceed to the next stage one step at a time and only when your pupil is happy.

Water immersion for the first time is a new experience for many individuals, and fear, lack of confidence or uncertainty are normal feelings.

Stage 1: Getting the face wet

Remember: getting the face wet and splashing in the face are two completely different concepts. The effects on pupils are not always positive ones. Here are a few practices to work through:

Blowing bubbles on the surface of the water or blowing an object along as they walk through the water is a great way to build confidence at this stage. Pupils can be encouraged to blow gently, like blowing through a straw, or blow with force, like blowing out candles on a cake.

Cupping water in their own hands and throwing it onto their face can further build confidence. This exercise works well in a group because it can encourage one or two particularly anxious pupils to copy their peers. It would help if you taught it in a fun way but, at the same time, did not force it on the nervous swimmer.

Stage 2: Partially submerging the face

Partial submersion is also best achieved with a gradual approach. Pupils first need to be taught to hold their breath by breathing in and keeping it all in. Some will be able to do this quickly, and others will learn by trial and error as they partially submerge their face and realise they cannot breathe underwater! Whatever the outcome, as a swimming teacher, you must treat these practices cautiously.

You can place an object just under the water surface, shallow enough for the pupil to see and reach for it but deep enough to submerge the mouth to get it. Once pupils have gained confidence with this exercise, you can lower the object slightly to encourage the mouth and nose to be submerged.

It is more effective to perform these practices with you, the teacher, holding the object yourself in the water. Having you teach from in the water may also help enhance pupils' confidence.

Stage 3: Total Submersion

Stage 2 naturally leads quickly onto stage 3, where you place the object below the water surface. The pupil is encouraged to retrieve it by completely submerging their head underwater. By this stage, breath-holding should be more accomplished, and the pupil should begin to relax more as they immerse.

Progression from this stage is to incorporate face submerging, wholly or partially, whilst swimming various strokes.

Standing From A Prone (Face Down) Position

Pupils can begin learning how to regain standing by holding the poolside or a float under each arm. As confidence grows, the swimmer can attempt standing without assistance, which requires greater use of the arms and hands. Pupils can also progress to a moving exercise, moving first towards and then away from the poolside.

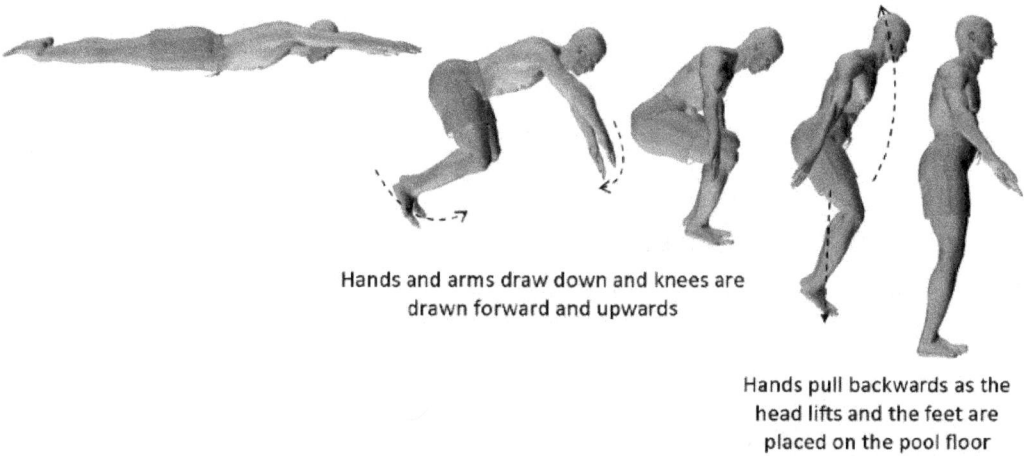

Hands and arms draw down and knees are drawn forward and upwards

Hands pull backwards as the head lifts and the feet are placed on the pool floor

Teacher's Focus
- Movement should be relaxed and smooth
- Draw the knees forward
- Arms pull downward and backwards
- The Head should lift and face forward

Teaching Points
- Pull down and back with both arms
- Bend knees forwards as if to sit
- Lift head upwards
- Place feet on the pool floor

Common Faults

- Rushed and not relaxed
- Failure to bend the knees
- Arching the back
- Failure to pull down and back

Standing From A Supine (Face Up) Position

Pupils can begin learning this by holding floats or having a woggle held under their arms. As confidence grows, the swimmer can attempt standing without assistance, which requires greater use of the arms and hands. Pupils can also progress this to a moving exercise.

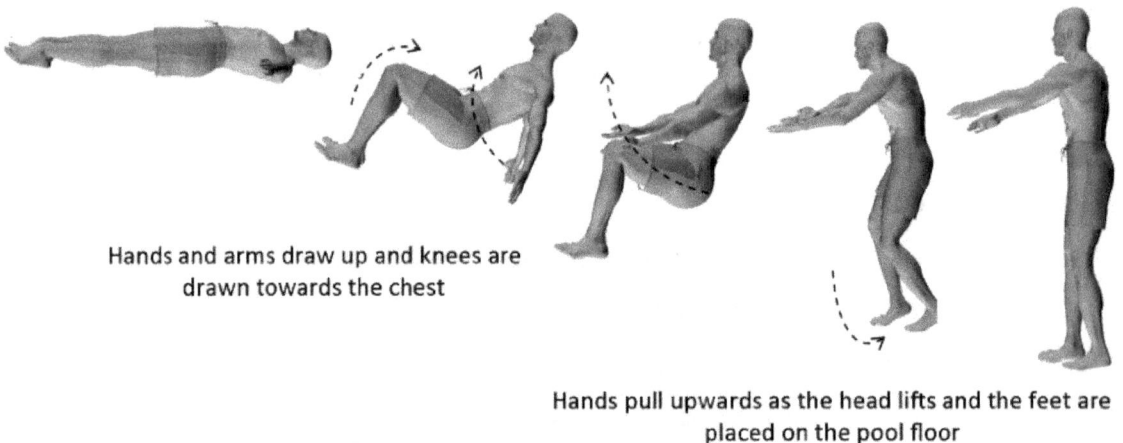

Hands and arms draw up and knees are drawn towards the chest

Hands pull upwards as the head lifts and the feet are placed on the pool floor

Teacher's Focus

- Movement should be relaxed and smooth
- Knees are drawn towards the chest
- Arms pull upwards and forwards
- The Head should lift and face forward

Teaching Points

- Pull both arms upwards to the surface
- Bend knees forwards as if to sit
- Lift head upwards
- Place feet on the pool floor

Common Faults

- Rushed and not relaxed
- Failure to bend the knees
- Arching the back
- Failure to pull up with both arms

The Psychology Of Floating

What your pupils might be thinking

It is typical for adults and those who fear water to think that the water is pulling them down. As a teacher, it is essential to educate your pupils that the water is trying to support them. The human body does not sink like a stone. Those that do not naturally float usually sink slowly and gradually.

So, with that in mind, we have to get our pupils into the mindset that they may have to move their arms and legs to help the water support them. Those movements can be very subtle, small ones. They may have to be more significant movements to help generate some momentum.

Either way, you have to encourage your pupils to do their bit to help the water support them. They will discover their level of buoyancy, which may not necessarily be at the water's surface.

What If They Naturally Sink?

The simple facts are that fat floats and muscle sinks. Therefore, fat people are better floaters than thin or muscular people.

Generally speaking, our legs are heavy and therefore sink. Our upper body will tend to float because our lungs contain air. But, the higher our body fat percentage, the better our chance of naturally staying afloat.

However, a lean or muscular pupil with a low body fat percentage can remain at the water surface as they swim, even though their body naturally wants to sink.

Relax and Glide And Floating Becomes Easier

Encourage your pupils to feel their way through the water, not fight it. Teaching them how to relax in the pool will erase tension as they discover how their bodies move and behave in water.

A gliding action through the water as they swim is key to learning how to relax. The momentum of a glide helps to remain at the water's surface and prevent sinking.

Gliding: the key to relaxing and floating

Gliding, in aquatic terms, is the concept of moving through the water, either at the surface or underwater, without assistance from arms or legs. It usually begins with a forceful push from the poolside or solid edge to generate some propulsion.

A streamlined body shape is vital for a glide to gain and maintain some distance.

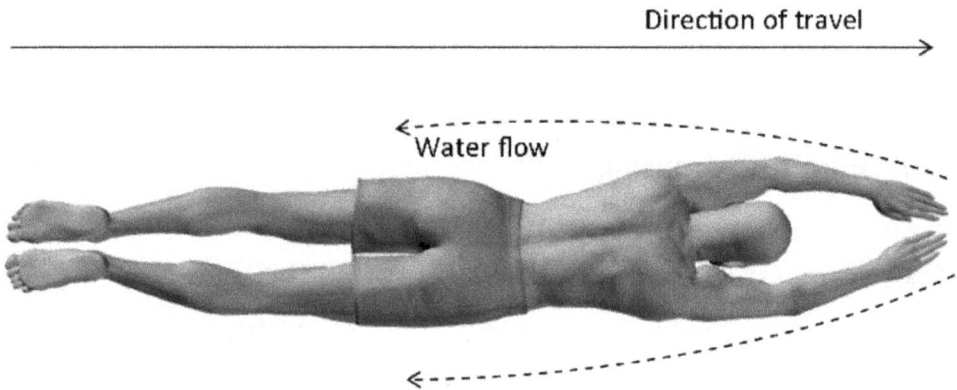

Direction of travel

Water flow

Emphasise to your pupils that personal body shape is not relevant here. We are not talking about how short, tall, fat or thin they are. Anyone's body shape can glide through the water. It is a matter of how pupils position their arms and legs as they glide.

Their hands and feet must be together to give a pointed, streamlined shape so that the water moves around them as their body cuts through it. If their hands and feet are apart, their body shape will create resistance and compromise movement through the water.

The first few glides can be scary

Some adults may find the thought of gliding through the water a scary one to begin with. They may feel wobbly and unbalanced as they move through the water unaided and without using their arms and legs.

Therefore, it is essential to start slowly. As your pupils get used to gliding, they can push away harder and glide further. Repetition is vital as they get used to how their body behaves in the water, which will help relax their body and mind.

Adults that are not natural floaters will begin to discover the point at which they start to sink as their glide begins to slow. They can also learn how fast they sink, which will be very slow, no matter how heavy they are.

As their glide slows and they begin to sink, we can teach them some basic movements to help maintain their glide and prevent sinking.

Basic Exercises To Build Confidence

All the exercises listed here are for pupils who have become confident with submerging their faces and breathing out into the water.

Wearing swim goggles will help to give a greater sense of awareness.

Exercise #1: Stationary floating

Floating in a stationary position does not come naturally to all pupils, and some will struggle. Nevertheless, practising floating is excellent for building confidence and making progress.

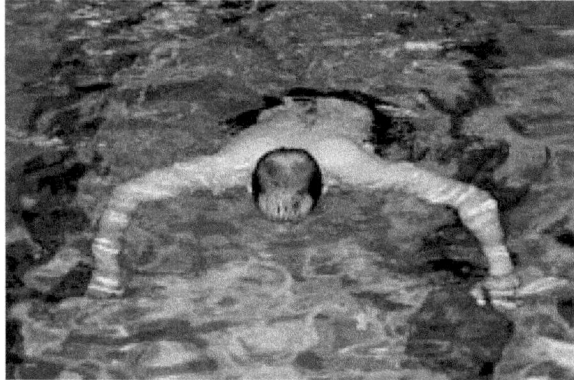

There are many ways to float, but the three best positions are:

- Star float (prone and supine)
- pencil float fully stretched (prone and supine)
- mushroom float

Star float

The pupil lies on the water's surface, with their arms and legs extended and opened into an 'X' shape. Pupils can perform a star float in a prone or supine position.

Pencil float

The pupil lies on the water's surface with arms extended alongside the body or above the head and fingers pointed. Their legs are extended, straight and together with the toes pointed. Pupils can perform a pencil float in a prone or supine position.

Mushroom float

The body is in a tucked position beneath the water's surface, the hands holding the lower leg somewhere between the ankle and knee; the chin and knees are held into the chest.

Exercise #2: push and glide

Teach your pupils to take a deep breath and push away from the pool wall. Demonstrate a stretched-out, streamlined position and encourage them to glide as far as they can in one breath.

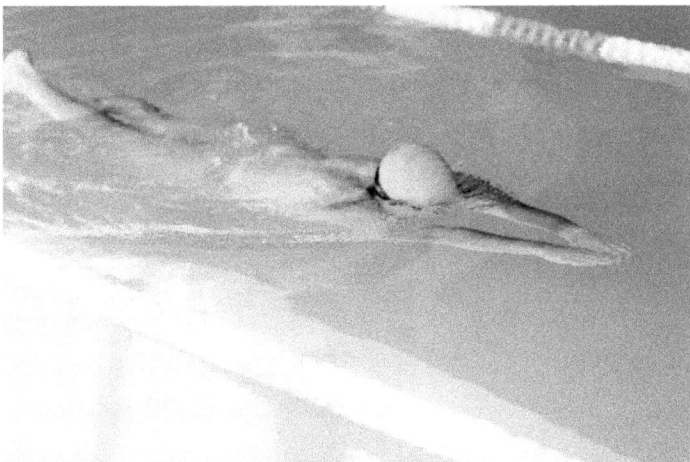

They may find themselves beginning to sink as momentum slows. Encourage your pupils to experiment and see what small movements of their legs, feet and hands can keep them moving and afloat.

Exercise #3: push and glide with kicks

This exercise is the same as #2 with a push and glide from the poolside. This time, leg kicks are added to help maintain momentum and prevent sinking.

The leg kicks can be alternating kicks, such as the kick used in front crawl or a simultaneous circular leg kick like the one used for breaststroke.

Exercise #4: push and glide on the back

Teach your pupils to perform a push and glide from the poolside in a supine (face-up) position. Ensure their head looks upwards, and their chest and hips are high up near the surface, and this will help enable their legs and feet to be at or near the water's surface.

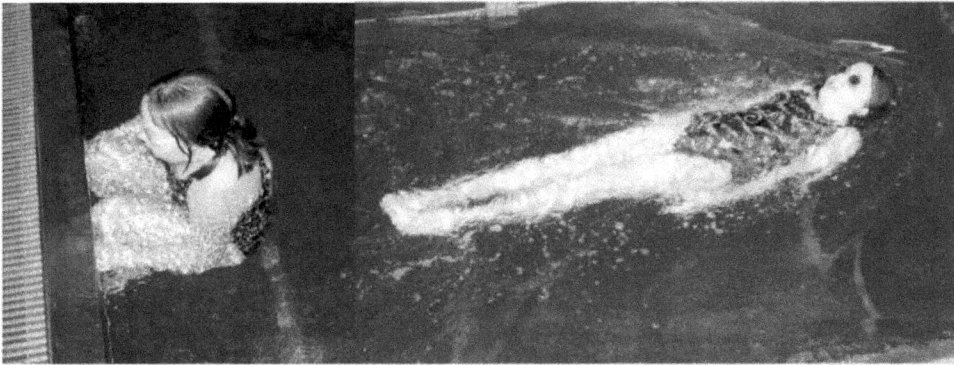

As the glide begins to slow, encourage them to use their hands by their sides in a sculling-type action (using the wrists to help the hands push water towards the feet) under the water. They can also use a gentle leg kick to maintain the movement and momentum through the water.

Treading Water

Treading water is a water skill that is a safe and controlled way of remaining at the surface in deep water, with the head above the water. It can be introduced to swimming lessons at a basic level even though it is not considered a basic swimming skill.

Learning how to tread water can be a massive confidence booster, particularly for adults, as it is an important swimming skill that can help conquer fears and anxieties and enhance and grow swimming strength in children and adults.

It is an effective way of building confidence in deep water and can enhance basic skills such as changing direction and avoiding collisions in the pool. It is also a vital lifesaving and survival skill.

How To Tread Water

Body Position

As treading water is a skill performed in one place (in other words, not swimming around), the body position should be as upright and vertical as possible.

Leg Kick

There are many variations of leg action when it comes to treading water. Some find it easier to 'cycle' in the water as the action is similar to riding a bicycle or running.

Different leg kicks include:

- Breaststroke - kicking in a downward action
- Alternating kick (similar to front crawl) - this is inefficient and tiring
- Scissor kick - similar to breaststroke but with an uneven action
- Egg beater kick - this is an alternating breaststroke kick and is the most efficient action

Arm Action

The main aim of the arm action when treading water is to help keep the body in a vertical position and keep the head above the water surface.

The movements of the arms should be underwater and relaxed at all times to help preserve energy. Techniques that pupils can use include:

- Breaststroke arm action - the basic arm technique, but adapted to include a slightly more downward action instead of the standard 'pull back'. The downward action results in an upward thrust, thus giving support when treading water.
- Sculling action - similar to breaststroke, the sculling arm action is just below the water surface and is continuous and relaxed. The hands and forearms perform a 'side-to-side' scooping type action with the palms facing downwards. The general action should provide a downward push, keeping the body lifted and supported.

Breathing and Timing

Breathing should be regular and steady, with the mouth and nose out of the water. All movements should be slow and relaxed, whichever arm and leg actions the pupil uses.

Teaching treading water

When teaching pupils how to tread water, all practices should take place in either shallow water or water of chest depth. Move your pupils into deeper water only when you are confident of their ability. Stay close to the side or have additional support in the form of a lifeguard or assistant teacher.

You might find the following exercise progression a useful guide:

- Standing in shallow water, practising the arm actions
- Using a woggle under the arms, practice the leg actions until you find the easiest one.
- Using a woggle in a 'seahorse' position, practising arm and leg actions
- Holding a float under each arm, practising the leg actions
- Without floats, sculling and lifting one leg off of the pool floor at a time
- Progress to deeper water without buoyancy aids

Front And Back Paddle

Front Paddle

Although breaststroke is considered one the best swimming strokes for adults to learn, some find that the front paddle comes more naturally. As adults practise other water confidence exercises, parts of front paddle are introduced, making this stroke a natural progression.

The front paddle is an alternating stroke, swimming in a horizontal prone position. Pupils can swim with their chin on the water surface or face submerged. The leg kick is an alternating, continuous action originating from the hips. The legs remain together as they kick, and pupils should point their toes with heels, just breaking the surface. The arms pull in an alternating action below the water's surface, stretching forward and pulling back with wrists firm and fingers together. Arm pulls will initially be short, and pupils should be encouraged to 'reach and pull' as they develop arm strength and confidence.

Pupils learning front paddle can be encouraged to blow bubbles across the water surface, enhancing their breathing confidence and breath control whilst pulling and kicking.

The whole stroke should be alternating and rhythmical, and pupils should be encouraged to increase the distance they swim front paddle to enhance their strength and stamina.

Possible exercises and drills to use when teaching front paddle include:

- push and glide from the poolside with buoyancy aids
- push and glide from the poolside without buoyancy aids
- kicking whilst holding the poolside
- kicking using a float under each arm
- kicking using one float held in both hands, progressing to swimming with the face in the water
- single arm pulls with a float held under one arm
- kicking and pulling using a woggle
- push and glide into full front paddle, kicking and pulling
- any of the above drills with added breathing technique and progressing to face in the water

Back Paddle

Back paddle is the first stroke on the back that beginners learn. Most adults will feel comfortable with back paddle because breathing is natural, and their face is clear of the water. Back paddle is also an ideal stroke to teach adults with limited shoulder movement and cannot swim backstroke.

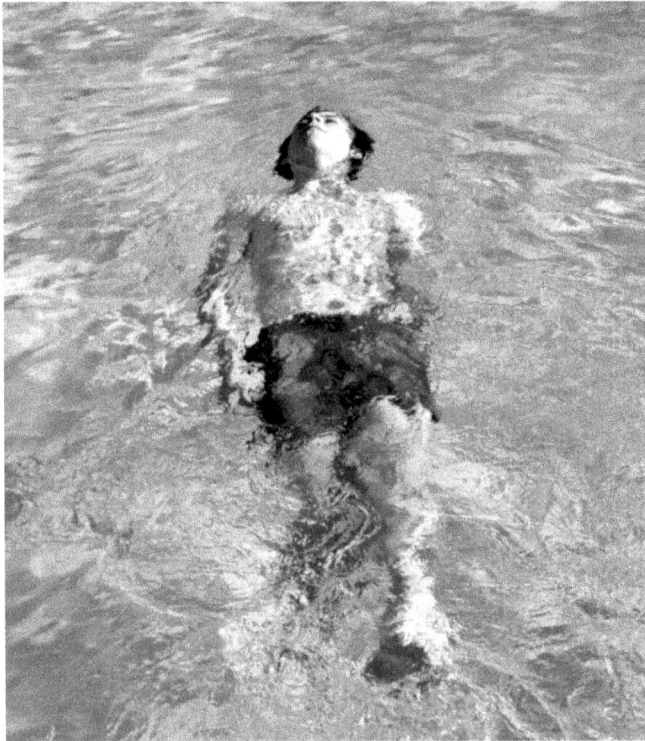

The body position for back paddle is horizontal and streamlined with an alternating and continuous leg kick and originates from the hips. Toes are pointed and ankles relaxed to help create a flipper-like kicking action. The upbeat of the kick generates propulsion, and the toes should break the surface of the water.

The arms remain straight and close to the body as they perform a sculling action with palms facing down, just under the water surface. Breathing should be natural, with all movements continuous and as relaxed as possible.

Possible exercises and drills to use when teaching back paddle include:

- supine push and glide from the poolside with buoyancy aids
- supine push and glide from the poolside without buoyancy aids
- kicking using a float or woggle under each arm
- kicking using one float held across the chest
- arm action with a woggle under the back
- kicking and pulling using a woggle
- supine push and glide into full back paddle, kicking and pulling

BLABT!

BLABT!

Teaching swimming strokes one part at a time

The most effective swimming teaching technique for teaching the four basic swimming strokes is **BLABT** – standing for:

Body position
Legs
Arms
Breathing
Timing

Teachers break down swimming strokes into these five parts, and pupils perform specific exercises or drills that focus on a particular area of their swimming technique.

For example, a BLABT breakdown for teaching front crawl stroke might look something like this:

- Body position – push and glide from the poolside.
- Legs – kicking whilst holding a kickboard or float out-stretched in front.
- Arms – practising arm pulls with one arm whilst holding a buoyancy aid with the other.
- Breathing – practising trickle breathing whilst holding a float and kicking
- Timing – front crawl catch-up, using a float or kickboard

Each of these five stroke parts can be taught in one single lesson so that the plan covers the whole stroke throughout the lesson. Alternatively, teachers can focus on one particular stroke part and spend the entire lesson fine-tuning it. They can then use a course of five or six lessons to teach each stroke part per lesson and use the final lesson to cover the full stroke again.

Exercises For Each Stroke Part

The exercises in this book are adult-friendly and cover the very basics of each swimming stroke. Each exercise focuses on a specific stroke part and lists teaching points for your pupils to focus on and common mistakes they might make as they swim.

The list of exercises is not definitive and exhaustive; there are no doubt many variations and others that are also appropriate and equally effective.

Some of the exercises are more difficult than others; therefore, as a swimming teacher, you must use your professional judgement to select the appropriate exercise and adapt it accordingly.

The exercises themselves are set out as a guide. Every adult is different and will interpret and respond to exercises and teaching points in their own way, so as a swimming teacher, it is important to be flexible in your approach. In other words, if a pupil finds a particular exercise difficult, adapt it to make it easier. If a pupil is not quite grasping the concept of what you are teaching, try using a different phrase or teaching point.

Teaching Points

Teaching points are our 'magic words'. Having a variety of them in our virtual tool kit can be extremely useful. For example, when you say to a pupil, *'point your toes, '* and they just don't get it, you change the teaching point to *'kick with floppy feet.'* All of a sudden, they are kicking with relaxed ankles and pointed toes.

Learning to be creative with our teaching points can be a very powerful skill and can be the difference between a pupil struggling and that light bulb moment when they suddenly understand and can do it.

Teaching Adults Breaststroke

Teaching Adults Breaststroke

Breaststroke is the perfect swimming stroke to teach adults because of its wide arm and leg movements that help build a sense of balance. Adults can also perform breaststroke with their face above the water and eyes looking forward, giving them a sense of security and balance.

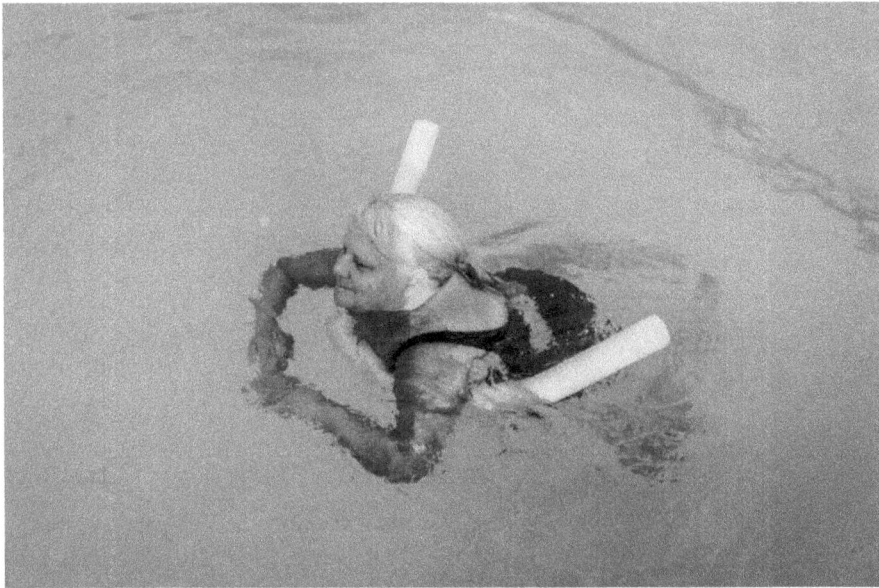

However, teaching adults how to swim breaststroke brings some barriers and limitations. These include:

Limited Flexibility

Generally speaking, adults lack flexibility all over, and the main areas requiring a significant degree of movement are the hips and ankles for swimming breaststroke. As a result, their leg action can often be quite limited, and restricted movement of the ankles can result in a lack of power in the overall leg kick.

An overall lack of flexibility can prevent the legs from being completely straight at the end of the power phase of the kick, and it can also limit the arms from stretching forward at the end of the recovery phase. The result can be an inefficient body shape during the glide phase.

Coordination

Many adults lack coordination and will find the 'pull-breath-kick-glide' sequence tricky to master. They will commonly attempt to pull and kick simultaneously and wonder why they seemingly go nowhere or, at best, travel through the water very slowly.

Add together these two most common limitations, and you have what most swimming teachers experience when teaching adults to swim - very slow progress.

Body Position

Static practice holding floats

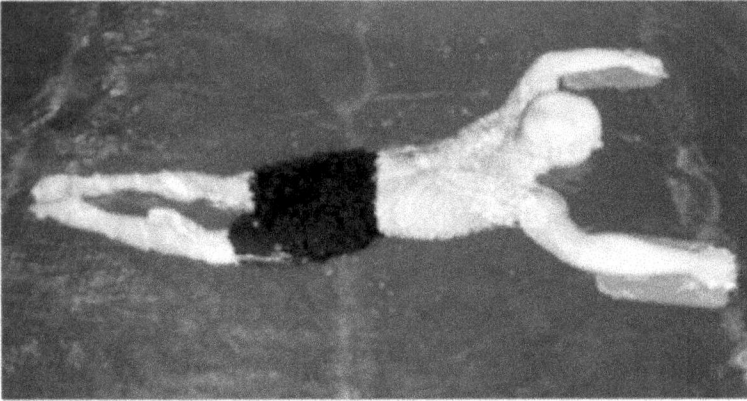

Aim: to help the swimmer develop confidence in their own buoyancy.

A float can be held under each arm or a single float held out in front, depending on levels of confidence and ability. Some swimmers may need extra assistance if they lack natural buoyancy.

Teaching Points

- Relax
- Keep the head tucked between the arms
- Stretch out as far as you can
- Keep your feet together

Teacher's Focus

- Head is central and still
- Face is submerged
- Eyes are looking downwards
- Shoulders should be level
- Hips are close to the surface
- Legs are together and in line with the body

Overall body position is horizontal and as flat
as possible

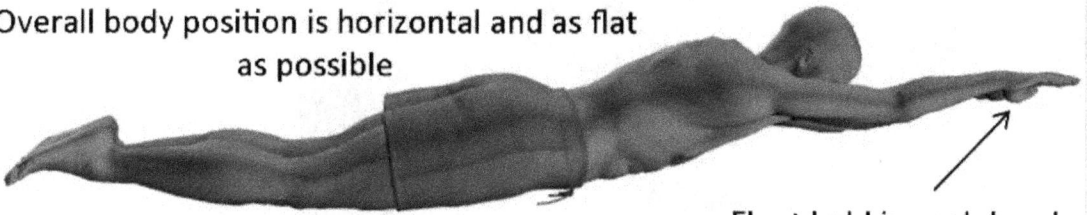

Float held in each hand
or single float held in
both hands

Common Faults	Remedy
Failure to submerge the face	Practice breathing and submersion exercises
Head is not central	Reiterate the teaching point and demonstrate
Whole body is not remaining straight	Reiterate the teaching point and demonstrate
Feet and hands are not together	Reiterate the teaching point and demonstrate

Legs

Prone position with a float held under each arm

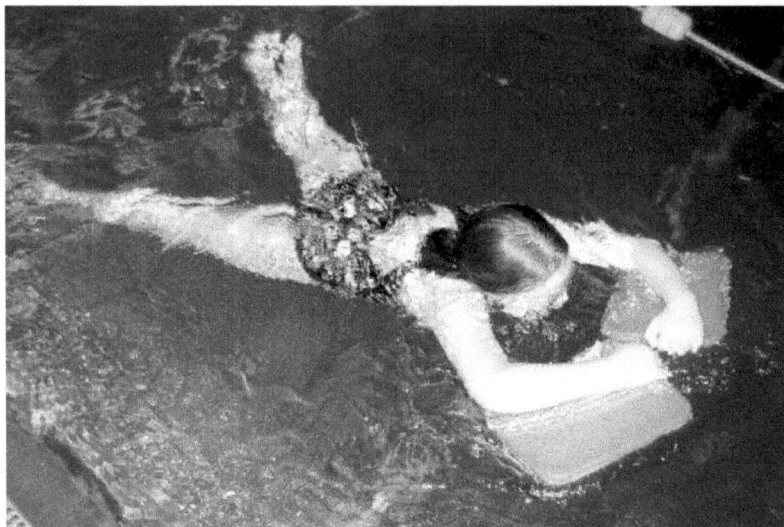

Aim: to practise and develop correct leg technique in a prone position.

Using two floats aids balance and stability and encourages correct body position whilst moving through the water.

Teaching Points

- Keep your knees close together
- Point your toes to your shins
- Drive the water backwards with your heels
- Glide with legs straight at the end of the each kick

Teacher's Focus

- Leg kick should be simultaneous
- Heels are drawn towards the seat
- The feet turn out just before the kick
- Feet kick back with knees inline with the hips
- Feet come together at the end of the kick

Prone position with a float held under each arm

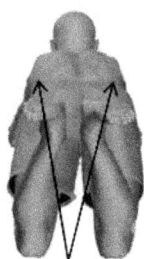

Heels are drawn up
towards the seat. Soles
face upwards

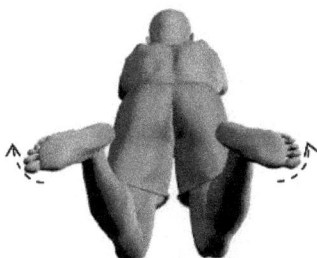

Feet turn outwards to allow the
heels and soles to aid propulsion

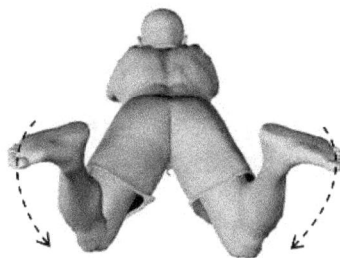

Heels push back and
outwards in a whip-like
action

Common Faults	Remedy
One foot turns out, causing a 'scissor' like kick	Practice slow kicking whilst sitting on the poolside
Legs kick back and forth	Reiterate the teaching point, demonstrate and practice
Legs kick is not simultaneous	Reiterate the teaching point, demonstrate and practice
Toes are not pointed at the end of the kick	Reiterate the teaching point, demonstrate and practice

Legs

Supine position with a woggle held under the arms

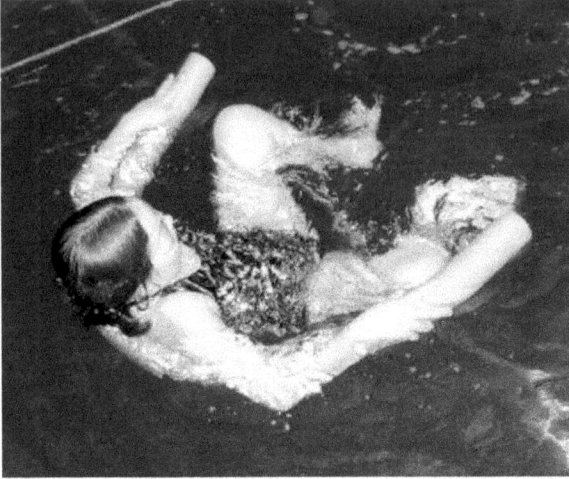

Aim: to develop breaststroke leg kick in a supine position.

This allows the swimmer to see their own legs kicking. The woggle provides stability for the beginner and, with the swimmer in a supine position, allows the teacher easy communication during the exercise.

Teaching Points

- Kick with both legs at the same time
- Keep your feet in the water
- Kick like a frog
- Kick and glide
- Point your toes at the end of the kick

Teacher's Focus

- Kick should be simultaneous
- Heels are drawn towards the seat
- The feet turn out just before the kick
- Feet kick back with knees just inline with the hips
- Feet come together at the end of the kick

Push and glide from the side holding floats

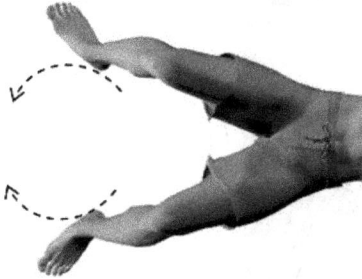

Heels drive back in a circular whip like action giving the kick power and motion

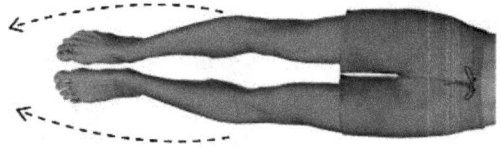

Kick finishes in a streamlined position with legs straight and toes pointed

Common Faults	Remedy
Feet are coming out of the water	Reiterate the teaching point and repeat
Failing to bring the heels up to the bottom	Repeat previous leg practice
Leg kick is not simultaneous	Reiterate teaching point and repeat
Legs are not straight at the end of the kick	Demonstrate and repeat

Legs

Holding a float out in front with both hands

Aim: to practise and learn correct kicking technique and develop leg strength.

Holding a single float or kickboard out in front isolates the legs and creates a slight resistance which demands a stronger kick with which to maintain momentum.

Teaching Points

- Drive the water backwards with force
- Turn your feet out and drive the water with your heels
- Kick and glide
- Kick like a frog
- Make your feet like a penguin

Teacher's Focus

- Kick should be simultaneous
- Legs drive back to provide momentum
- Heels are drawn towards the seat
- The feet turn out before the kick
- Feet come together at the end of the kick with legs straight and toes pointed

Holding a float out in front with both hands

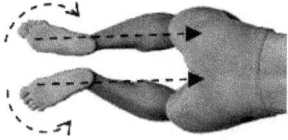

Heels drawn towards the seat and feet turn out

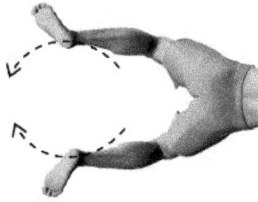

Heels drive back in a circular whip like action giving the kick power and motion

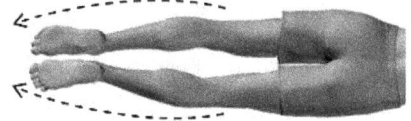

Kick finishes in a streamlined position with legs straight and toes pointed

Common Faults	Remedy
Kick is slow and lacking power	Repeat earlier leg practices
Failing to bring the heels up to the bottom	Repeat earlier leg practices
Feet are breaking the water surface	Check the body position and correct
Toes are not pointed at the end of the kick	Reiterate the teaching point and repeat

Legs

Moving practice with arms stretched out in front

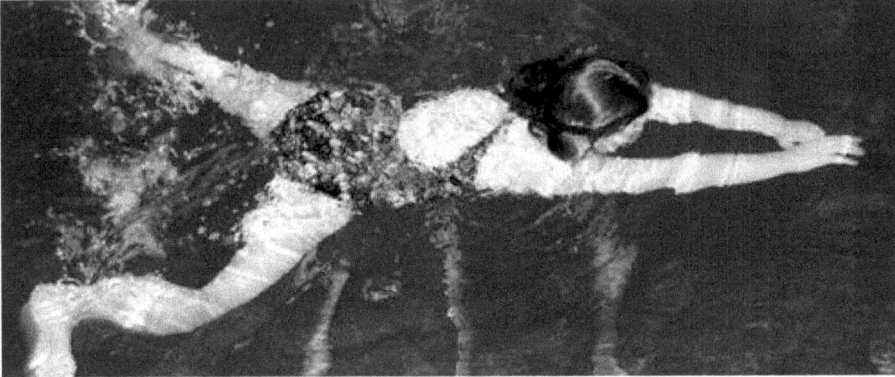

Aim: to practise correct kicking technique and develop leg strength.

This is an advanced exercise as holding the arms out in front demands a stronger kick with which to maintain momentum whilst maintaining a streamlined body position.

Teaching Points

- Keep your knees close together
- Drive the water with your heels
- Make sure your legs are straight at the end of the kick
- Kick and glide

Teacher's Focus

- Kick should be simultaneous
- The feet turn out just before the kick
- Feet kick back with knees just inline with the hips
- Feet come together at the end of the kick with legs straight and toes pointed

Moving practice with arms stretched out in front

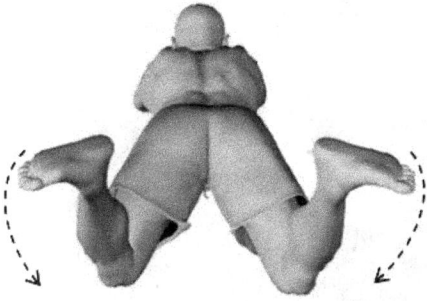

Heels push back and outwards in a
whip-like action

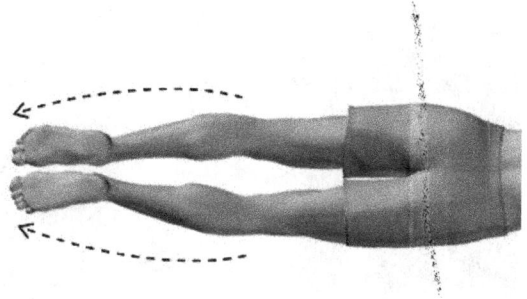

Kick finishes in a streamlined position
with legs straight and toes pointed

Common Faults	Remedy
Not turning both feet out	Reiterate the teaching point, demonstrate and practice
Feet are breaking the water surface	Check the body position or revert to earlier exercises
Legs are not straight at the end of the kick	Revert to earlier leg kick practices
Toes are not pointed at the end of the kick	Revert to earlier leg kick practices

Arms

Walking practice moving through shallow water

Aim: to practise and develop correct arm technique from in the water.

The swimmer can experience the feel of pulling the water whilst walking along the pool floor. Where the water is too deep, this exercise can be performed standing on the poolside. Submerging the face is optional at this stage.

Teaching Points

- Pull with both arms at the same time
- Keep your hands under the water
- Tuck your elbows into your sides after each pull
- Stretch your arms forward until they are straight
- Draw an upside down heart with your hands

Teacher's Focus

- Arm action should be simultaneous
- Arms and hands should remain under water
- Fingers should be together
- Arms should extend forward and together until straight after each pull

Walking practice moving through shallow water

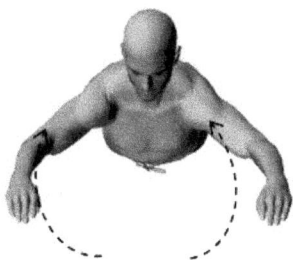

Arms and hands pull back in a
circular motion

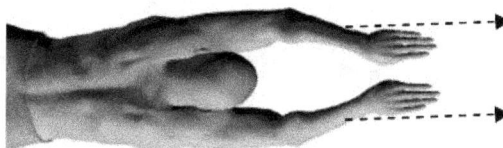

Elbows tuck in and arms and hands stretch
forward into a glide

Common Faults	Remedy
Fingers are too wide apart	Reiterate the teaching point, demonstrate and practice
Arms pull past the shoulders	Demonstrate and repeat
Elbows fail to tuck in each time	Demonstrate and repeat
Arms fail to extend full forward	Reiterate the teaching point, demonstrate and practice
Hands come out of the water	Reiterate the teaching point, demonstrate and practice

Arms

Moving practice with a woggle held under the arms

Aim: to learn correct arm action whilst moving through the water.

The use of the woggle means that leg kicks are not required to assist motion and this then helps develop strength in the arm pull. The woggle slightly restricts arm action but not enough to negate the benefits of this exercise.

Teaching Points

- Pull round in a circle
- Keep your hands under the water
- Keep your fingers together and hands flat
- Pull your body through the water
- Draw an upside down heart with your hands

Teacher's Focus

- Arm action should be simultaneous
- Arms and hands should remain under water
- Arms and hands should extend forward after the pull
- Fingers should be together
- Arm pull should be circular

Moving practice with a woggle held under the arms

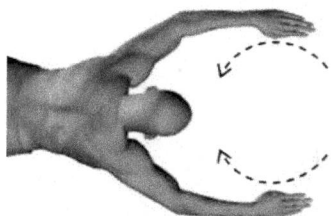

Arms and hands pull around
and downwards

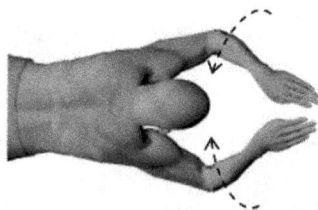

Elbows tuck in and arms and hands stretch
forward into a glide

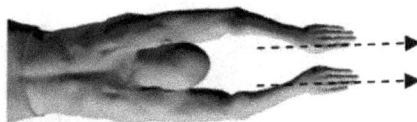

Common Faults	Remedy
Fingers are too wide apart	Repeat earlier arm practices
Arms fail to extend fully forward	Demonstrate and repeat
Hands come out of the water	Reiterate the teaching point and repeat
Arms extend forward too far apart	Reiterate the teaching point and repeat

Arms

Push and glide adding arm pulls

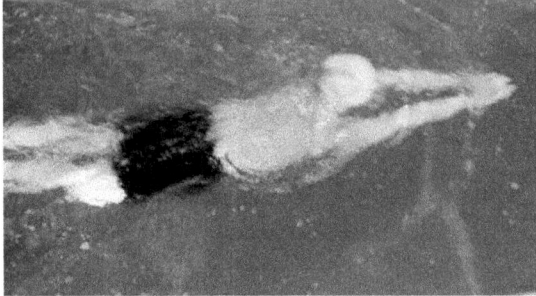

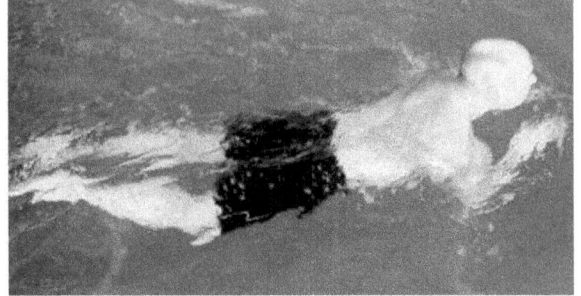

Aim: to progress arm action and technique from previous exercises.

By incorporating a push and glide, this allows the swimmer to practise maintaining a correct body position whilst using the arms. This is a more advanced exercise as the number of arms pulls and distance travelled will vary according to the strength of the swimmer.

Teaching Points

- Keep your hands under the water
- Pull your body through the water
- Tuck your elbows into your sides after each pull
- Stretch your arms forward with hands together

Teacher's Focus

- Arms and hands should remain under water
- Elbows should be tucked in after each pull
- Arms should extend forward into a glide position
- Body position should be maintained throughout

Direction of travel

Water flow

Arms and hands pull around
and downwards

Arms and hands
stretch forward into
the original glide
position

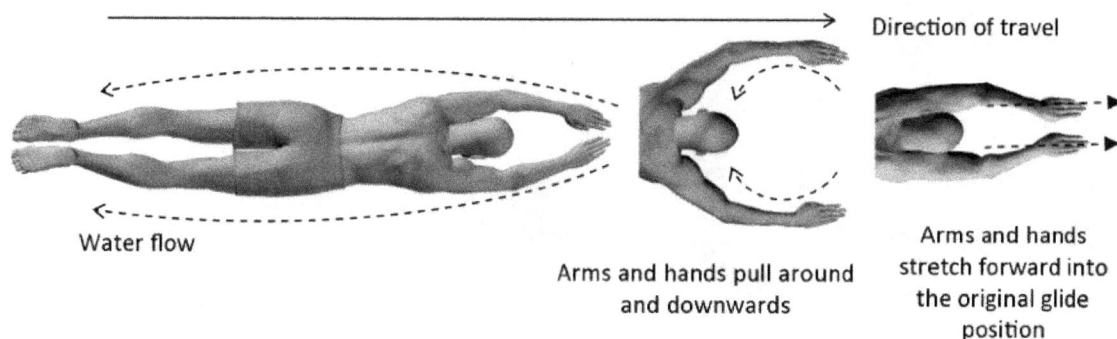

Common Faults	Remedy
Arms pull past the shoulders	Revert to the previous arm practice
Arms fail to extend full forward	Reiterate the teaching point, demonstrate and practice
Hands come out of the water	Repeat earlier arm practices
Arms extend forward too far apart	Reiterate the teaching point and repeat
Arms fail to bend during the pull	Repeat earlier arm practices

Breathing

Static practice, breathing with arm action

Aim: to practise breaststroke breathing action whilst standing in the water.

This allows the swimmer to experience the feel of breathing into the water in time with the arm action, without the need to actually swim.

Teaching Points

- Breathe in as you complete your arm pull
- Breathe out as your hands stretch forwards
- Blow your hands forwards

Teacher's Focus

- Breath inwards at the end of the in sweep
- Head lifts up as the arms complete the pull
- Head should clear the water
- Head returns to the water as the arms recover
- Breath out is as the hands recover forward

Push and glide adding arm cycles

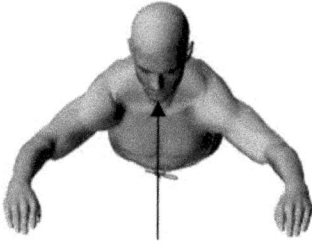

Breathe IN as the arms pull
down and the head rises

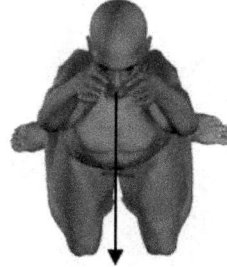

Breathe OUT as the arms recover
forward and the face enters the
water

Common Faults	Remedy
Head fails to clear the water	Reiterate the teaching point, demonstrate and practice
Breathing out as the arms pull back	Reiterate the teaching point, demonstrate and practice
Lifting the head to breathe as the arms recover	Reiterate the teaching point, demonstrate and practice

Breathing

Breathing practice with woggle under the arms

Aim: to develop correct synchronisation of breathing and arm pull technique.

The woggle provides support, which enables the exercise to be done slowly at first. It also allows the swimmer to travel during the practice. Leg action can be added if necessary. Note: the woggle can restrict complete arm action.

Teaching Points

- Breathe in as you complete your arm pull
- Breathe out as your hands stretch forwards
- Blow your hands forwards

Teacher's Focus

- Breath inwards at the end of the in-sweep
- Head lifts up as the arms complete the pull back
- Head should clear the water
- Head returns to the water as the arms recover
- Breathing out is as the hands stretch forward

Breathing practice with woggle under the arms

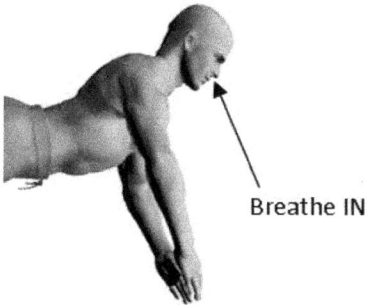

Breathe IN

Breathing in occurs as the arms pull down and
the head rises above the surface

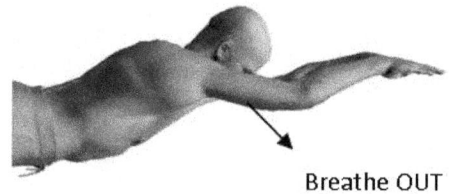

Breathe OUT

Breathing out occurs as the arms recover
out in front

Common Faults	Remedy
Holding the breath	Revert to previous basic breathing exercises to encourage breathing out
Head fails to clear the water	Revert to previous basic breathing exercises to encourage breathing out
Breathing out as the arms pull back	Revert to previous basic breathing exercises to encourage breathing out
Lifting the head as the arms stretch forward	Reiterate the teaching point, demonstrate and practice

Breathing

Float held in front, breathing with leg kick

Aim: to develop the breathing technique in time with the leg kick.

The float provides stability and allows the swimmer to focus on the breathe kick glide action.

Teaching Points

- Breathe in as your legs bend ready to kick
- Breathe out as you kick and glide
- Kick your head down

Teacher's Focus

- Inward breathing should be just before the knees bend
- Head lifts up as the knees bend ready to kick
- Mouth should clear the water
- Head returns to the water as the legs thrust backwards
- Breathe out is as the legs kick into a glide

Breathing
Float held in front, breathing with leg kick

Breathe IN just before the knees bend for the kick

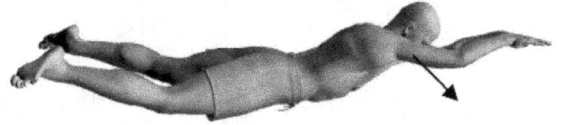

Breathe OUT as the legs kick into a glide

Common Faults	Remedy
Holding the breath	Revert to previous basic breathing exercises to encourage breathing out
Head fails to clear the water	Revert to earlier breathing practices
Breathing out as the knees bend ready to kick	Reiterate the teaching point and repeat
Lifting the head as the legs kick into a glide	Reiterate the teaching point and repeat

Timing

Slow practice with woggle under the arms

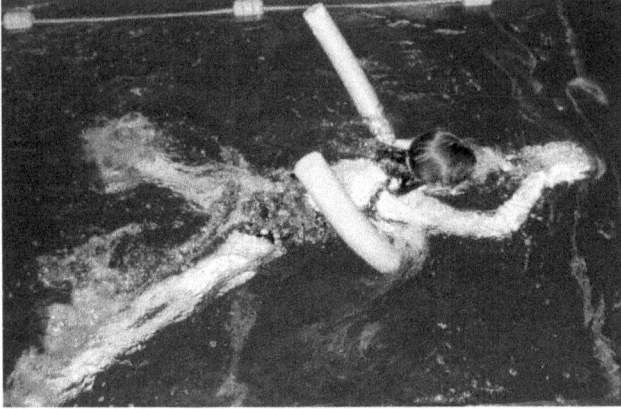

Aim: to practise the stroke timing in its most basic form.

The use of the woggle placed under the arms allows the swimmer to practice the exercise in stages as slowly as they need. It must be noted that the woggle resists against the glide and therefore the emphasis must be placed on the timing of the arms and legs. The glide can be developed using other exercises.

Teaching Points

- Pull with your hands first
- Kick your hands forwards
- Kick your body into a glide
- Pull, breathe, kick, glide

Teacher's Focus

- From a streamlined position arms should pull first
- Legs should kick into a glide
- Legs should kick as the hands and arms recover
- A glide should precede the next arm pull

Timing
Slow practice with woggle under the arms

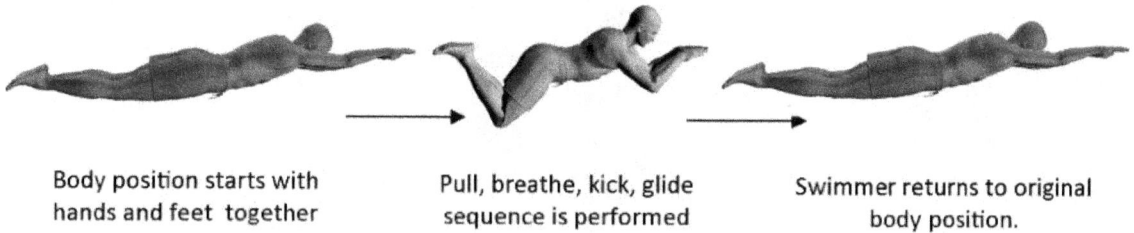

Body position starts with hands and feet together

Pull, breathe, kick, glide sequence is performed

Swimmer returns to original body position.

Common Faults	Remedy
Kicking and pulling at the same time	Reiterate the teaching point, demonstrate and practice
Failure to glide	Reiterate the teaching point, demonstrate and practice
Legs kick whilst gliding	Reiterate the teaching point, demonstrate and practice

Timing

Push and glide, adding stroke cycles

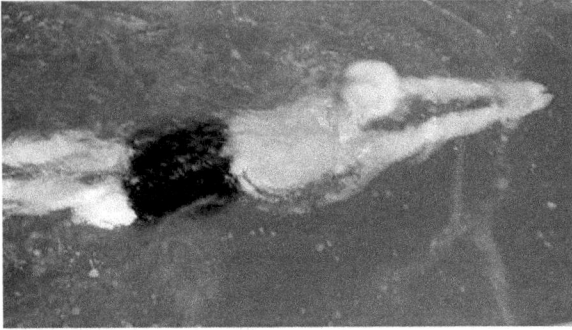

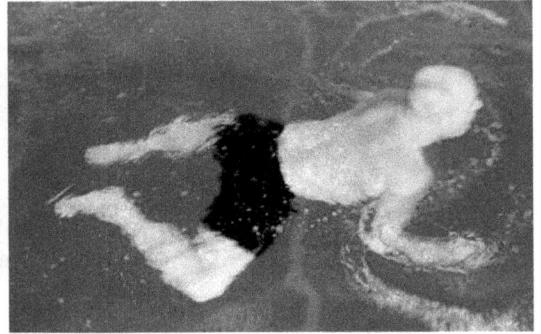

Aim: to practise and develop correct stroke timing.

The swimmer starts with a push and glide to establish a streamlined glide. The arm pull, breath in and then leg kick is executed in the correct sequence, resulting in another streamlined glide.

Teaching Points

- Kick your hands forwards
- Kick your body into a glide
- Pull, breathe, kick, glide

Teacher's Focus

- From a streamlined position arms should pull first
- Legs should kick into a glide
- Legs should kick as the hands and arms recover
- A glide should precede the next arm pull

Water flow ←- - - - - - - - - - - - - - - - -

Push and glide to establish body position

Pull, breathe, kick and glide again

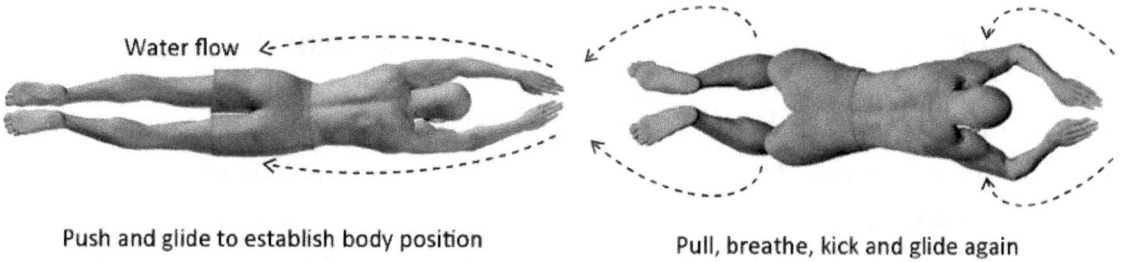

Common Faults	Remedy
Kicking and pulling at the same time	Repeat previous timing practice
Failure to glide	Reiterate the teaching point and repeat
Legs kick whilst gliding	Reiterate the teaching point and repeat

Full Stroke

Aim: to swim full stroke Breaststroke demonstrating efficient arm and leg action, with regular breathing and correct timing.

Teaching Points

- Kick and glide
- Kick your hands forwards
- Drive your feet backward through the water
- Keep your fingers together and under the water
- Pull in a small circle then stretch forward
- Breath with each stroke

Teacher's Focus

- Head remains still and central
- Shoulders remain level
- Leg kick is simultaneous
- Feet turn out and drive backwards
- Arm action should be circular and simultaneous
- Breathing is regular with each stroke cycle

Common Faults	Remedy
Failure to glide	Repeat earlier timing practices
Stroke is rushed	Encourage a longer glide and repeat
Leg kick is not simultaneous	Repeat earlier leg practices
Arms pull to the sides	Repeat earlier arm practices
Failing to breath regularly	Repeat earlier breathing practices

Teaching Adults Front Crawl

Teaching Adults Front Crawl

Teaching adults how to swim front crawl brings its barriers and limitations. These include:

Joint Flexibility

Generally speaking, adults lack flexibility all over, so the main area that requires a significant degree of movement is the shoulders when swimming front crawl. As a result, their arm action can often be quite limited. Arm pulls might be shortened, recovery over the water is often wide of the shoulder line, with much less elbow bend, and hand and arm entry can lack a stretch forward.

The other area where adults often lack flexibility is in their ankles, which can affect the leg kick by preventing the feet and toes from pointing as they kick, making the overall kick inefficient and causing drag. A lack of movement in the ankles also means losing the relaxed flipper-like action as they kick.

These areas' lack of flexibility often makes for a very inefficient swimming stroke.

Fitness and Stamina

Whilst a lack of general fitness and stamina is not always the case for adults in the swimming pool, learning to swim front crawl could be a relatively new challenge, so it is fair to say they lack 'swimming fitness'. They could be a regular marathon runner or accomplished long-distance cyclist but still be utterly exhausted after swimming one length of front crawl, which is very common.

Add together these two most common limitations, and you have what most swimming teachers experience when teaching adults to swim - very slow progress.

Body Position

Static practice holding floats

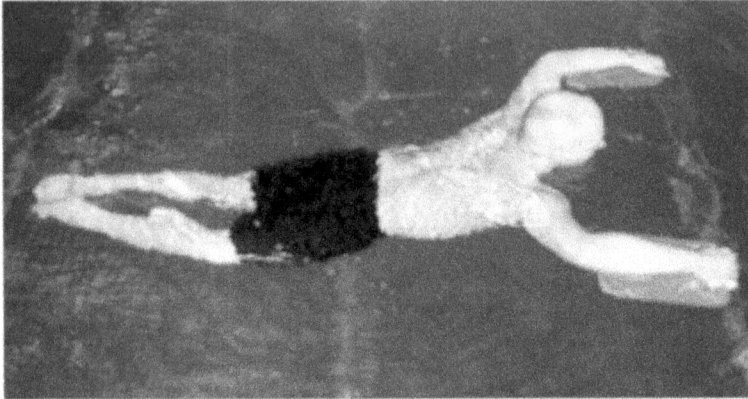

Aim: to help the swimmer develop confidence in his/her own buoyancy.

A float can be held under each arm or a single float held out in front, depending on levels of confidence and ability. Some swimmers may need extra assistance if they lack natural buoyancy.

Teaching Points

- Relax
- Keep the head tucked between the arms
- Stretch out as far as you can
- Keep your feet together

Teacher's Focus

- Head is central and still
- Face is submerged
- Eyes are looking downwards
- Shoulders should be level
- Hips are close to the surface
- Legs are together and in line with the body

Overall body position is horizontal and as flat
as possible

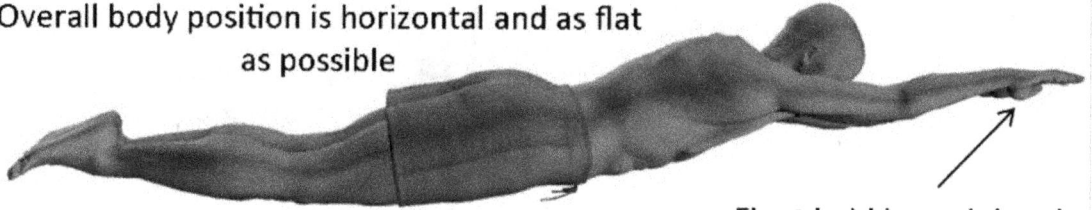

Float held in each hand
or single float held in
both hands

Common Faults	Remedy
Failure to submerge the face	Practice breathing and submerging exercises to build confidence
Head is not central	Reiterate the teaching point and demonstrate
Whole body is not remaining straight	Reiterate the teaching point and demonstrate
Feet and hands are not together	Reiterate the teaching point and demonstrate

Body Position

Push and glide from standing

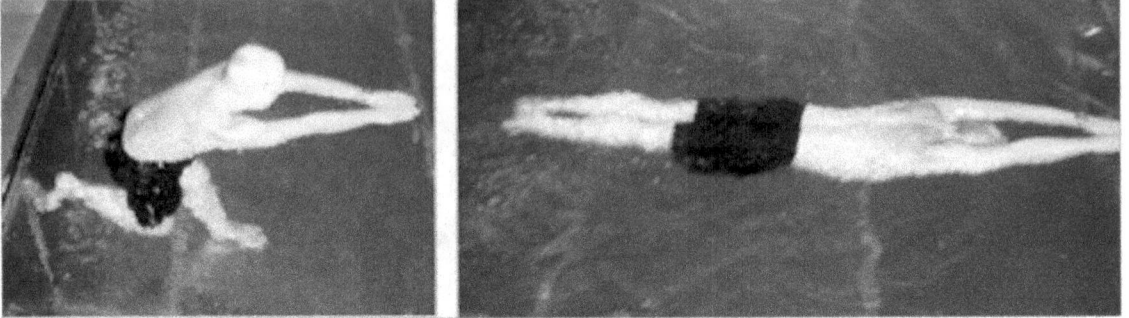

Aim: to develop correct body position and confidence in pushing off.

The swimmer can start with arms stretched out in front and pushes off from the pool floor or from the wall with one foot and glides through the water unaided.

Teaching Points

- Push hard from the side/pool floor
- Keep your head tucked between your arms
- Stretch out as far as you can
- Keep your hands together
- Keep your feet together

Teacher's Focus

- Initial push should be enough to gain good movement
- Head remains still and central
- Face submerged so that the water is at brow level
- Shoulders should be level
- Legs in line with the body

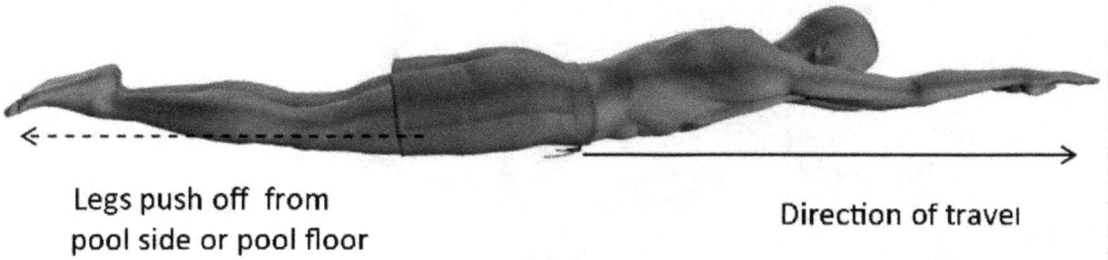

Legs push off from
pool side or pool floor

Direction of travel

Common Faults	Remedy
Failure to submerge the face	Revert to previous exercises
Push off is too weak	Reiterate the teaching point and demonstrate
Whole body is not remaining straight	Reiterate the teaching point and demonstrate
Feet and hands are not together	Reiterate the teaching point and demonstrate

Body Position

Push and glide from the side holding floats

Aim: to develop correct body position whilst moving through the water.

Body position should be laying prone with the head up at this stage. The use of floats helps to build confidence, particularly in the weak or nervous swimmer. The floats create a slight resistance to the glide, but this is still a useful exercise.

Teaching Points

- Push hard from the wall
- Relax and float across the water
- Keep your head still and look forward
- Stretch out as far as you can
- Keep your feet together

Teacher's Focus

- Head remains still and central with the chin on the water surface
- Eyes are looking forwards and downwards
- Shoulders should be level and square
- Hips are close to the surface
- Legs are in line with the body

Push and glide from the side holding floats

Water flow

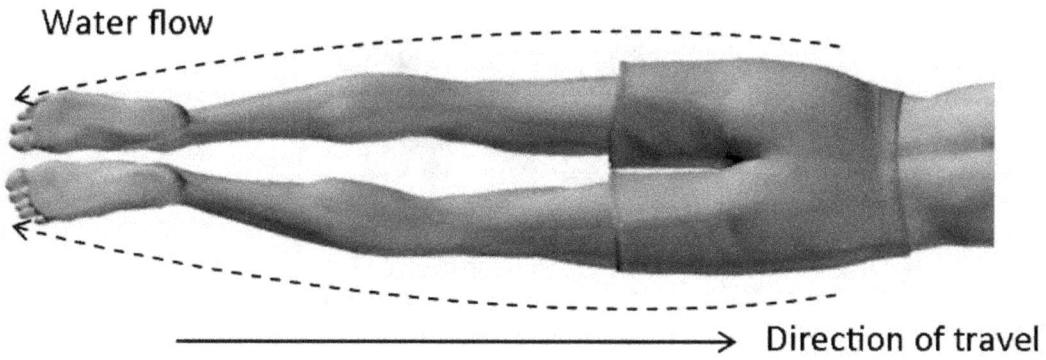

Direction of travel

Common Faults	Remedy
Push from the side is not hard enough	Revert to previous exercises
Head is not central	Reiterate the teaching point and demonstrate
Whole body is not remaining straight	Reiterate the teaching point and demonstrate
Feet are not together	Reiterate the teaching point and demonstrate

Body Position

Push and glide from the poolside

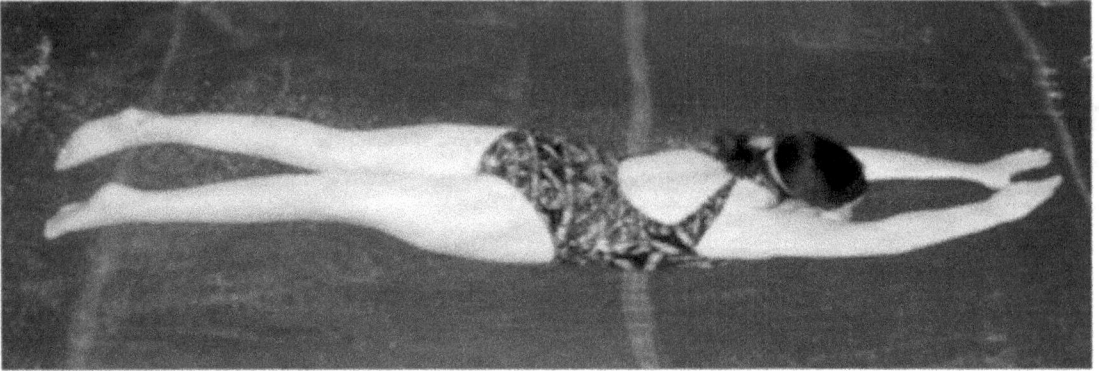

Aim: to develop a streamlined body position whilst moving thorough the water.

Movement is created by pushing and gliding from holding position at the poolside.

Teaching Points

- Head remains still and central
- Face submerged so that the water is at brow level
- Shoulders should be level and square
- Legs are in line with the body
- Overall body position should be streamlined

Teacher's Focus

- Push hard from the side
- Stretch your arms out in front as you push
- Keep your head tucked between your arms
- Stretch out as far as you can
- Keep your hands and feet together

Water flow
←- -

————————————————→ Direction of travel

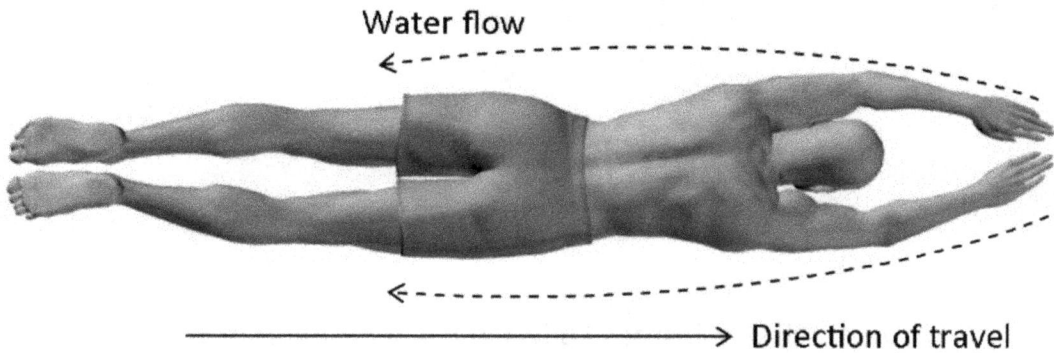

Streamlined body position minimises drag, allowing efficient movement
through the water

Common Faults	Remedy
Push from the side is too weak	Reiterate the teaching point and repeat
Arms stretch in front *after* the push	Standing practice with arms in front
Head is not central	Reiterate the teaching point and repeat
Feet are not together	Reiterate the teaching point and demonstrate
Overall body position not in line	Revert to the previous exercise

Legs

Holding the poolside

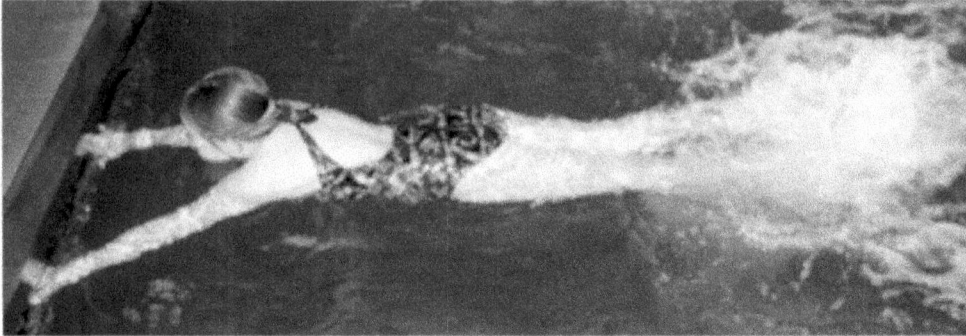

Aim: to encourage the swimmer to learn the kicking action.

Holding the poolside enhances confidence and helps develop leg strength and technique.

Teaching Points

- Kick with straight legs
- Pointed toes
- Make a small splash with your toes
- Kick with floppy feet
- Kick from your hips
- Kick continuously
- Legs kick close together

Teacher's Focus

- Kick comes from the hip
- Kick is continuous and alternating
- Knee is only slightly bent
- Legs are close together when they kick
- Ankles are relaxed and the toes are pointed
- Kick should just break the water surface

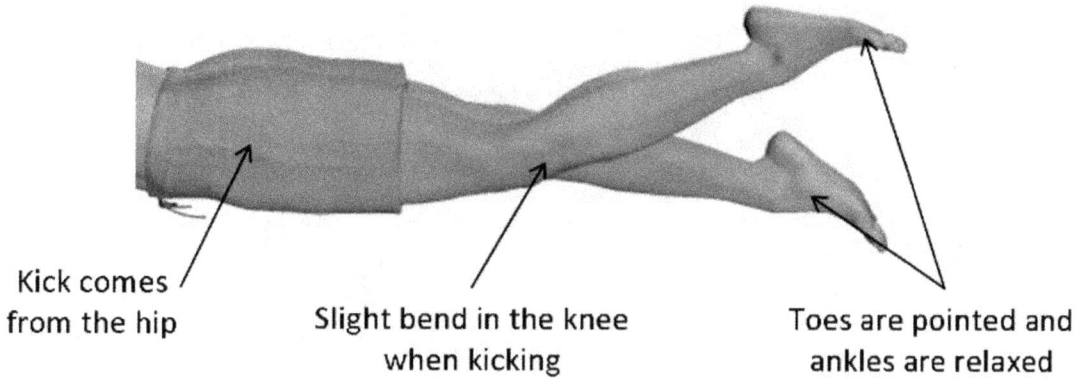

Kick comes from the hip

Slight bend in the knee when kicking

Toes are pointed and ankles are relaxed

Common Faults	Remedy
Feet come out of the water	Check the body position and repeat
Kick comes from the knee	Reiterate the teaching point, demonstrate and practice
Legs are too deep in the water	Check the body position and correct

Legs

Legs kick with a float held under each arm

Aim: to learn correct kicking technique and develop leg strength.

The added stability of two floats will help boost confidence in the weak swimmer.

Teaching Points

- Kick with straight legs
- Pointed toes
- Kick with floppy feet
- Kick from your hips
- Kick continuously

Teacher's Focus

- Kick comes from the hip
- Kick is continuous and alternating
- Chin remains on the water surface
- Legs are close together when they kick
- Ankles are relaxed and the toes are pointed
- Kick should just break the water surface
- Upper body and arms should be relaxed

Legs
Legs kick with a float held under each arm

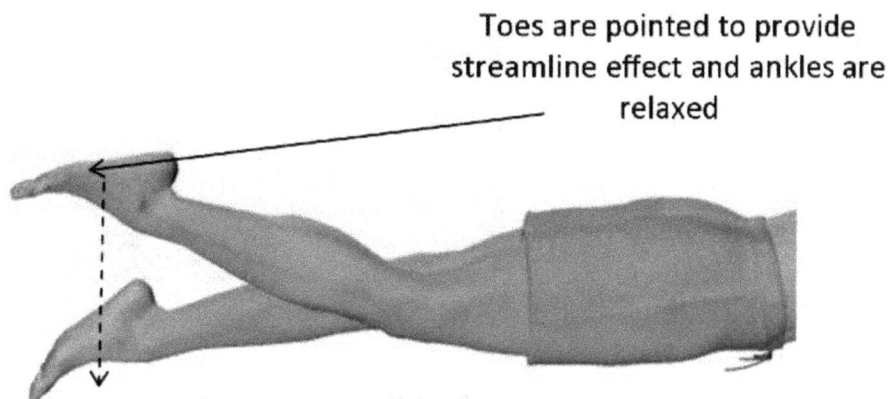

Toes are pointed to provide streamline effect and ankles are relaxed

Downward kick provides propulsion

Common Faults	Remedy
Head lifts above the surface, causing the legs to sink	Encourage face submersion
Kick comes from the knee causing excessive bend	Reiterate the teaching point or revert back to a previous exercise
Kick is not deep enough	Encourage kicking from the hips
Legs are too deep in the water	Check the body position and correct

Legs

Float held with both hands

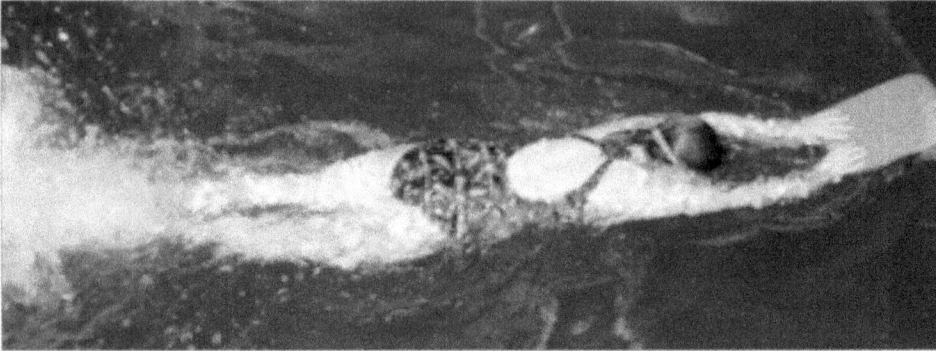

Aim: to practise and learn correct kicking technique.

Holding a float or kickboard out in front isolates the legs, encourages correct body position and develops leg strength.

Teaching Points

- Kick with pointed toes
- Make a small splash with your toes
- Kick with floppy feet
- Legs kick close together

Teacher's Focus

- Kick comes from the hip
- Kick is continuous and alternating.
- Legs are close together when they kick
- Ankles are relaxed and the toes are pointed.
- Kick should just break the water surface

Toes are pointed to provide streamline effect
and ankles are relaxed

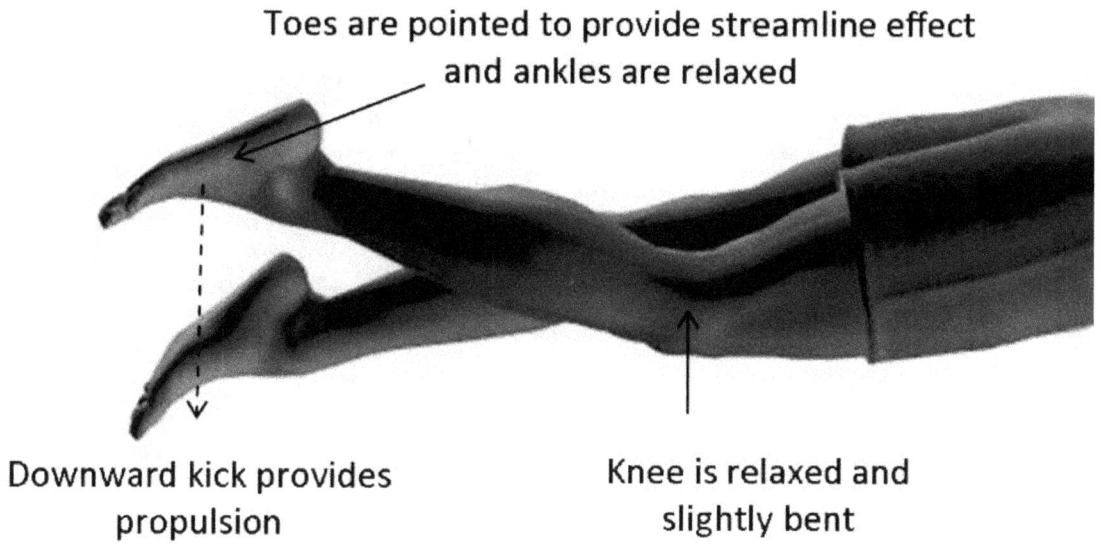

Downward kick provides
propulsion

Knee is relaxed and
slightly bent

Common Faults	Remedy
Knees bend too much	Revert to earlier leg practices
Feet come out of the water	Check the body position
Kick comes from the knee	Reiterate the teaching point, demonstrate and practice
Legs are too deep in the water	Revert to earlier body position practices

Legs

Push and glide with added leg kick

Aim: to develop correct body position and leg kick whilst holding the breath.

Push and glide without a float and add a leg kick whilst maintaining a streamlined body position.

Teaching Points

- Kick with straight legs and pointed toes
- Kick with floppy feet
- Kick from your hips
- Kick continuously

Teacher's Focus

- Kick comes from the hip
- Streamlined body position is maintained
- Kick is continuous and alternating
- Legs are close together when they kick
- Ankles are relaxed and the toes are pointed
- Kick should just break the water surface

Kick comes from the hip

Relaxed knees
and ankles

Body position remains level

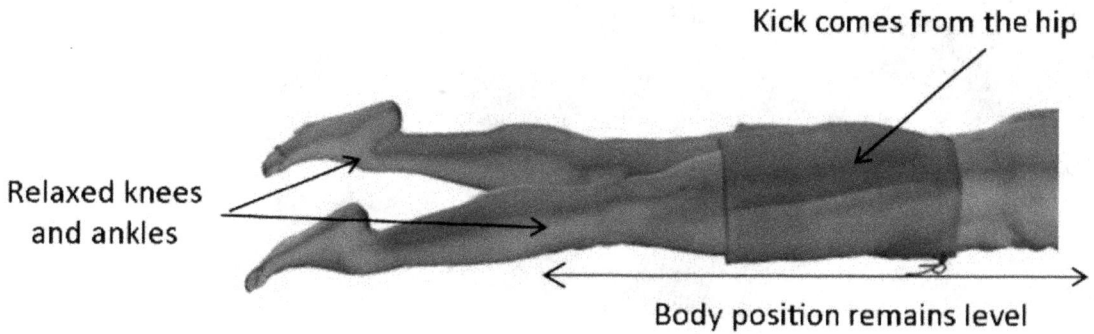

Common Faults	Remedy
Ankles are not relaxed	Revert to earlier leg practices
Feet come out of the water	Check the body position or revert to earlier exercises
Kick is not deep enough	Reiterate the teaching point, demonstrate and practice
Legs are too deep in the water	Revert to earlier body position practices

Arms

Single arm practice with float held in one hand

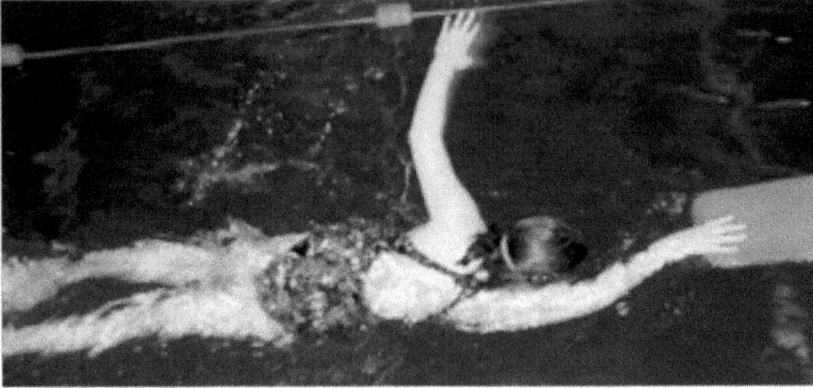

Aim: to practise and improve correct arm technique.

This practice allows the swimmer to develop arm technique whilst maintaining body position and leg kick. Holding a float with one hand gives the weaker swimmer security and allows the competent swimmer to focus on a single arm.

Teaching Points

- Keep your fingers together
- Brush your hand past your thigh
- Pull fast under the water
- Make an 'S' shape under the water
- Elbow out first
- Reach over the water surface

Teacher's Focus

- Fingertips enter first with thumb side down
- Fingers should be together
- Pull should be an elongated 'S' shape
- Pull through to the hips
- Elbow exits the water first
- Fingers clear the water on recovery

Single arm practice with float held in one hand

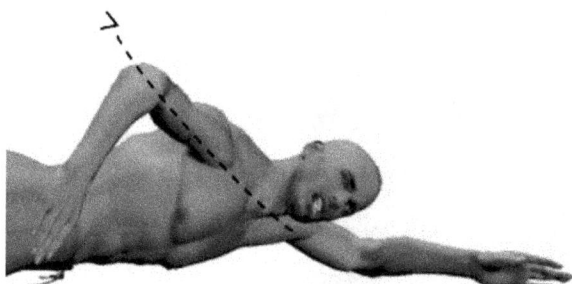

Elbow leads out of the
water first

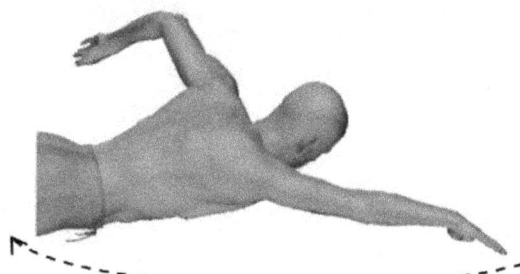

Arm pulls back through the water
towards the hip

Common Faults	Remedy
Fingers are too wide apart	Reiterate the teaching point, demonstrate and practice
Pull is short and not to the thigh	Revert to the previous arm practice
Lack of power in the pull	Further arm exercises to build strength and stamina
Arm pull is too deep underwater	Revert to the previous arm practice
Arms are too straight on recovery	Repeat the static standing practice

Arms

Alternating arm pull whilst holding a float out in front

Aim: to develop coordination and correct arm pull technique.

The swimmer uses an alternating arm action. This also introduces a timing aspect, as the leg kick has to be continuous at the same time.

Teaching Points

- Finger tips in first
- Brush your hand past your thigh
- Pull fast under the water
- Elbow out first
- Reach over the water surface

Teacher's Focus

- Clean entry with fingertips first and thumb side down
- Fingers should be together
- Each arm pulls through to the hips
- Elbow leads out first
- Fingers clear the water on recovery

Arms
Alternating arm pull whilst holding a float out in front

Arm pulls through towards the hip

Elbow leads high and the hand follows over the water surface

Common Faults	Remedy
Fingers are too wide apart	Reiterate the teaching point, demonstrate and practice
Pull is short and not to the thigh	Revert to the previous arm practice
Lack of power in the pull	Further arm exercises to build strength and stamina
Hand entry is wide of shoulder line	Revert to the previous arm practice
Arms are too straight on recovery	Repeat the static standing practice

Arms

Push and glide adding arm cycles

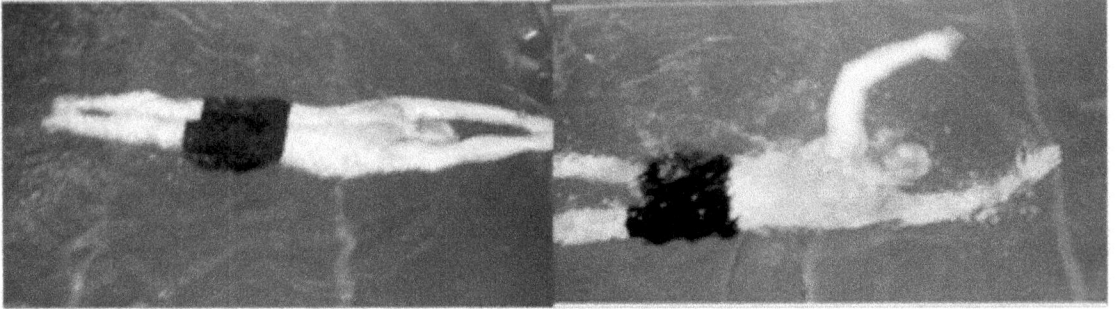

Aim: to combine correct arm action with a streamlined body position.

The swimmer performs a push and glide to establish body position and then adds arm cycles, whilst maintaining body position.

Teaching Points

- Finger tips in the water first
- Brush your hand past your thigh
- Make an 'S' shape under the water
- Elbow out first
- Reach over the water surface

Teacher's Focus

- Clean entry with fingertips first
- Pull should be an elongated 'S' shape
- Pull through to the hips
- Elbow comes out first
- Fingers clear the water on recovery

Push and glide establishes
correct body position

Arm cycles are added

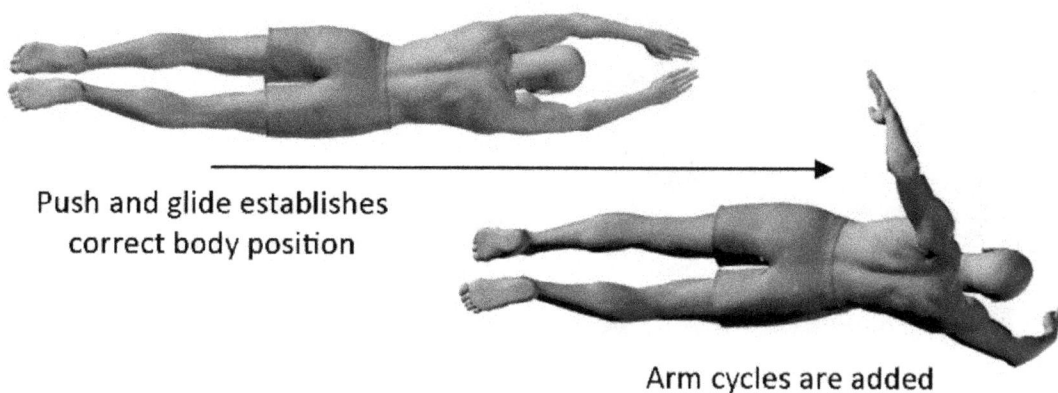

Common Faults	Remedy
Arms are too straight under water	Reiterate the teaching point, demonstrate and practice
Pull is short and not to the thigh	Revert to the previous arm practice
Lack of power in the pull	Further arm exercises to build strength and stamina
Hand entry is across the centre line	Repeat the earlier standing practice
Arms are too straight on recovery	Repeat the static standing practice

Breathing

Standing and holding the poolside

Aim: to practice and develop breathing technique.

The pupil stands and holds the pool rail with one arm extended, breathing to one side to introduce the beginner to breathing whilst having his/her face submerged.

Teaching Points

- Breathe out through your mouth
- Blow out slowly and gently
- Turn your head to the side when you breathe in
- See how long you can make the breath last

Teacher's Focus

- Breathing should be from the mouth
- Breathing in should be when the head is turned to the side
- Breathing out should be when the face is down

BREATHE IN

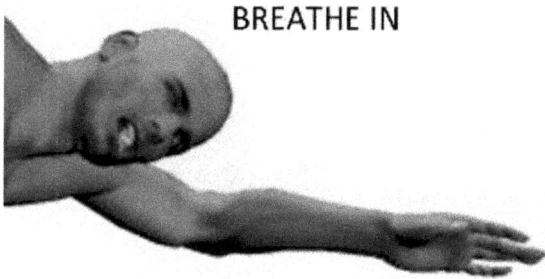

Head turns to the side and mouth clears the water surface

BREATHE OUT

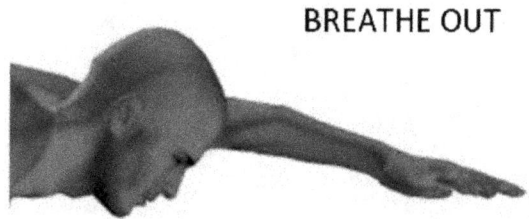

Head faces forward and down

Common Faults	Remedy
Breathing through the nose	Reiterate the teaching point, demonstrate and practice
Holding the breath	Revert to previous basic breathing exercises to encourage breathing out

Breathing

Holding a float in front with diagonal grip

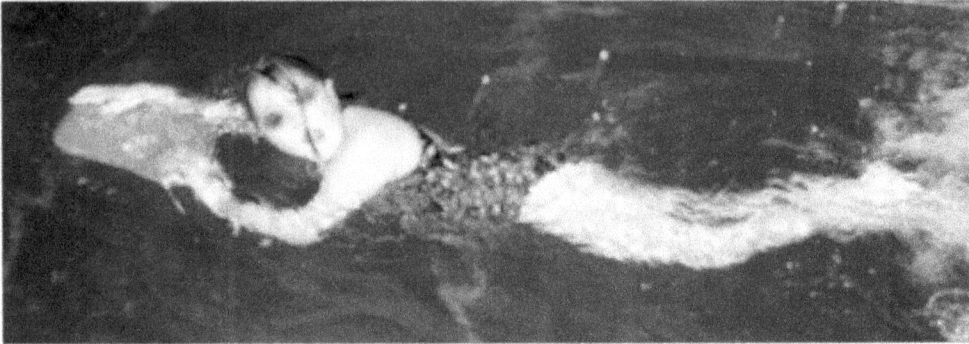

Aim: to encourage correct breathing technique whilst kicking.

The float is held in front; one arm extended fully, the other holding the near corner with elbow low. This creates a gap for the head and mouth to be turned in at the point of breathing.

Teaching Points

- Turn head towards the bent arm to breathe
- Breathe out through your mouth
- Blow out slowly and gently
- Return head to the centre soon after breathing

Teacher's Focus

- Breathing should be from the mouth
- Breathing in should be when the head is turned to the side
- Breathing out should be slow and controlled

Breathing
Holding a float in front with diagonal grip

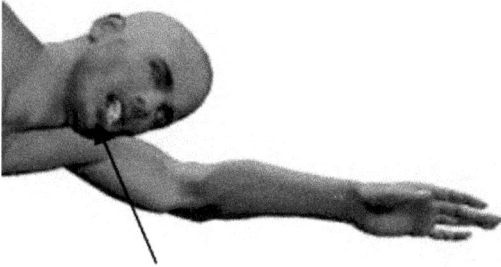

Breathe IN as the head turns
out of the water

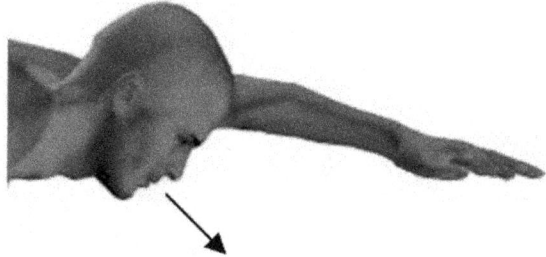

Breathe OUT as the head
faces forward and down

Common Faults	Remedy
Breathing through the nose	Reiterate the teaching point, demonstrate and practice
Holding the breath	Revert to previous basic breathing exercises to encourage breathing out
Lifting the head and looking forward	Reiterate the teaching point, demonstrate and practice
Turning towards the straight arm	Reiterate the teaching point, demonstrate and practice

Breathing

Float held in one hand, arm action with breathing

Aim: to develop correct breathing technique whilst pulling with one arm.

This allows the swimmer to add the arm action to the breathing technique and perfect the timing of the two movements. The float provides support and keeps the exercise as a simple single arm practice.

Teaching Points

- Turn head to the side of the pulling arm
- Breathe out through your mouth
- Blow out slowly and gently
- Return head to the centre soon after breathing

Teacher's Focus

- Head moves enough for mouth to clear the water
- Breathing in occurs when the head is turned to the side
- Breathing out should be slow
- Breathing should be from the mouth

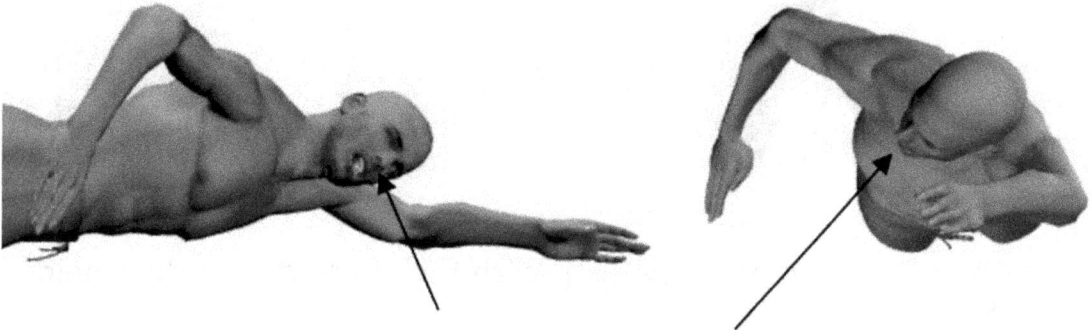

Breath IN as the arm pulls through and the head turns to the side

Common Faults	Remedy
Breathing through the nose	Reiterate the teaching point, demonstrate and practice
Holding the breath	Revert to previous basic breathing exercises to encourage breathing out
Lifting the head and looking forward	Revert to earlier breathing practices
Turning towards the straight arm	Revert to earlier breathing practices
Turning the head too much	Revert to earlier breathing practices

Breathing

Float held in both hands, alternate arm pull with breathing

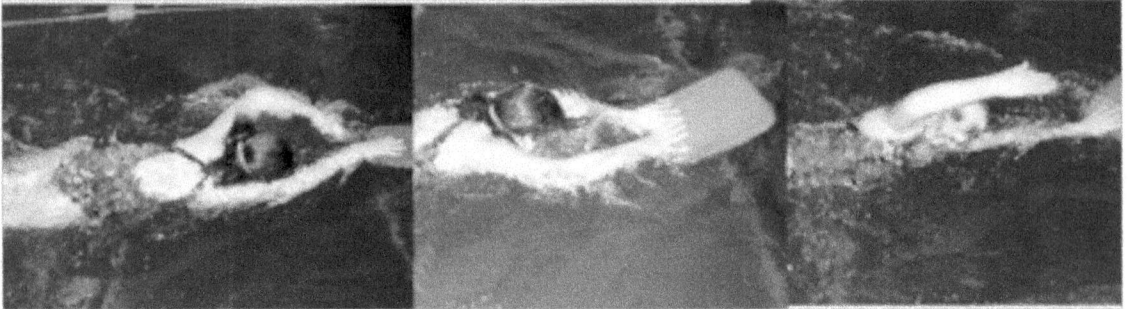

Aim: to practise bi-lateral breathing with the support of a float held out in front.

A single float is held in both hands and one arm pull is performed at a time with the head turning to breathe with each arm pull. Different arm action and breathing cycles can be used, for example; breathe every other arm pull or every three arm pulls.

Teaching Points

- Keep head still until you need to breathe
- Breathe every 3 strokes (or another pattern you may choose)
- Turn head to the side as your arm pulls back
- Return head to the centre soon after breathing
- Breathe out through your mouth

Teacher's Focus

- Head should be still when not taking a breath
- Head movement should be minimal enough for mouth to clear the water
- Breathing in should be when the head is turned to the side
- Breathing should be from the mouth

Breathing
Float held in both hands, alternate arm pull with breathing

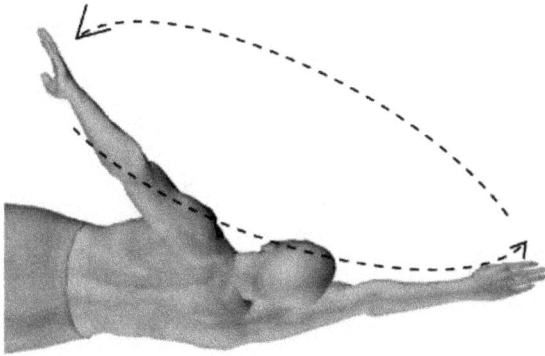

Head turns to the left side as the left arm pulls through and begins to recover

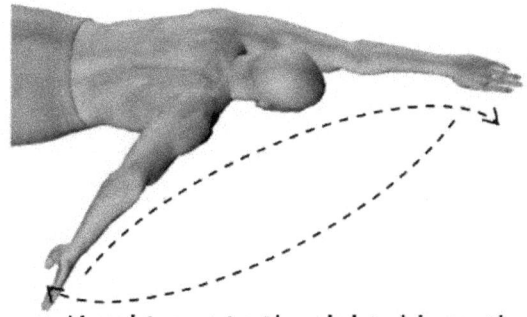

Head turns to the right side as the right arm pulls through and begins to recover

Common Faults	Remedy
Turning the head too early or late to breath	Reiterate the teaching point, demonstrate and practice
Lifting the head and looking forward	Revert to earlier breathing practices
Turning towards the straight arm	Revert to earlier breathing practices
Turning the head too much	Revert to earlier breathing practices

Full Stroke

Aim: full stroke Front Crawl demonstrating correct leg action, arm action, breathing and timing.

Teaching Points

- Keep your head still until you breathe
- Kick continuously from your hips
- Stretch forward with each arm action
- Pull continuously under your body
- Count 3 leg kicks with each arm pull

Teacher's Focus

- Stroke is smooth and continuous
- Head in line with the body
- Legs in line with the body
- Head remains still
- Leg kick is continuous and alternating
- Arm action is continuous and alternating
- Breathing is regular and to the side
- Stroke ideally has a 6 beat cycle

Common Faults	Remedy
Head moves from side to side	Revert to previous arm practices
Legs kick from the knee	Repeat earlier leg practices
Leg action is too slow	Repeat earlier leg practices
Arm action is untidy and splashing	Repeat earlier arm practices
Excessive head movement when breathing	Repeat previous breathing practices
Head is lifted, causing legs to sink	Repeat body position practices
Stroke is erratic and rushed	Check timing and encourage to swim slower

Teaching Adults Backstroke

Teaching Adults Backstroke

Most adults will need some intervention when learning to swim on their back. Learning to swim in a supine position will test their confidence, ability to float and awareness of their surroundings.

Although backstroke is a natural progression from back paddle, teaching adults how to swim backstroke does bring some common barriers and limitations. These include:

Lack of Flexibility

When it comes to swimming backstroke, the main area that requires a significant degree of movement is the shoulders. As a result, their arm action can often be limited. Arm pulls might become shortened due to their inability to stretch up fully so that the arm brushes past the ear. Adult backstroke arms often enter the water at an angle, wide of the body line.

Another area where adults often lack flexibility is their ankles, which can affect the leg kick by preventing the feet and toes from pointing as they kick. The lack of ankle movement can make the overall kick inefficient and cause drag. A lack of movement in the ankles also means losing the relaxed flipper-like action as they kick. This lack of flexibility can result in either an excessive knee bend as they kick or their feet and legs gradually sinking, compromising the overall body position.

Lack of Confidence

When learning to swim front crawl, breaststroke or any other method on the front, swimmers can see where they are going and the water surface, the poolside and the pool floor. In short, they have total awareness of where they are and what they are doing. This awareness and perception is removed when learning to swim on the back, significantly affecting confidence.

Body Position

Floating supine supported by floats

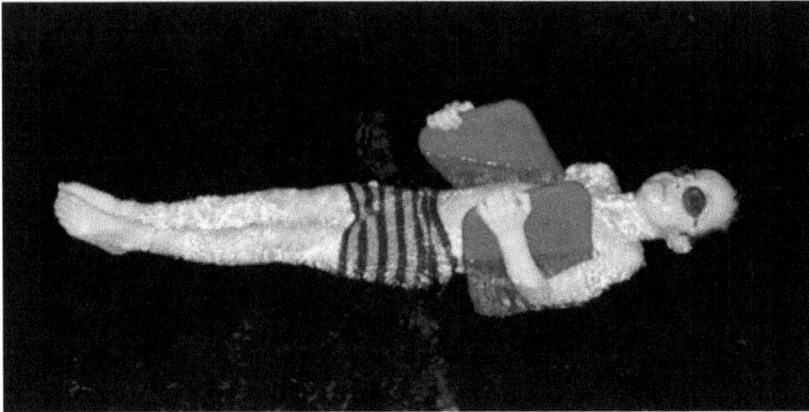

Aim: to gain confidence in a supine position on the water surface.

This exercise is ideal for the nervous swimmer. Support initially can be provided by the teacher or assistant, if he/she is also in the water. 2 floats can then provide support, one placed under each arm, or by a woggle placed under both arms as in the photograph above.

Teaching Points

- Relax
- Make your body flat on top of the water
- Keep your head back
- Push your tummy up to the surface
- Look up to the ceiling
- Keep your head still
- Keep yourself in a long straight line

Teacher's Focus

- Overall body should be horizontal and streamlined
- Head remains still
- Eyes looking upwards and towards the feet
- Hips must be close to the surface
- Legs must be together

Body position remains level

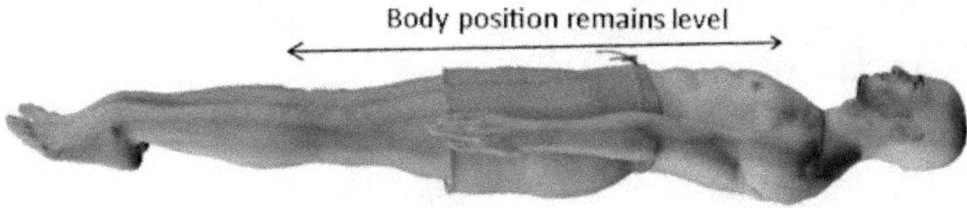

Common Faults	Remedy
Head raises out of the water	Reiterate the teaching point
Waist and hips sink	Reiterate the teaching point
Failing to maintain a flat position	Assist and encourage relaxation

Body Position

Static supine position, holding a single float

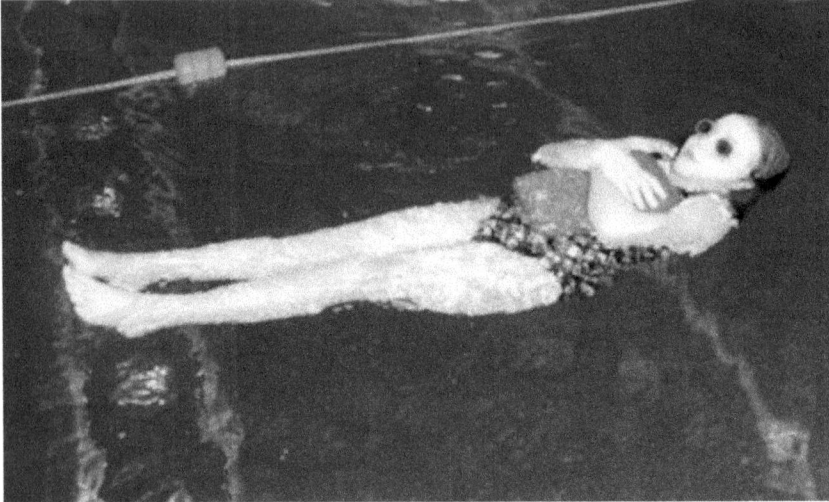

Aim: to develop confidence in a supine position.

Holding a single float across the chest gives security to the nervous swimmer, but is not as stable as a woggle or a float under each arm and so is a subtle and gradual progression. If necessary, this exercise can be performed without a float, as shown in the diagram below, as an additional progression.

Teaching Points
- Relax
- Keep your head back
- Push your tummy up to the surface
- Look up to the ceiling
- Keep your head still

Teacher's Focus
- Overall body should be horizontal
- Head remains still
- Eyes looking upwards
- Hips must be close to the surface
- Legs must be together

Body Position
Static supine position, holding a single float

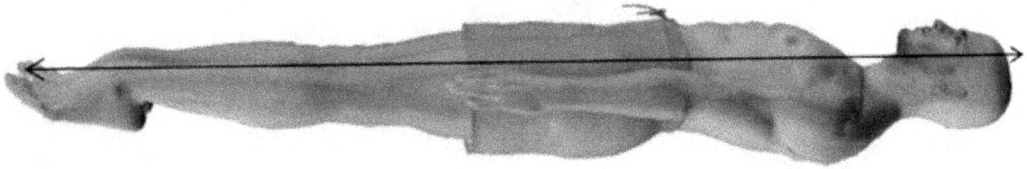

Body position remains horizontal and relaxed

Common Faults	Remedy
Head raises out of the water	Reiterate the teaching point and repeat
Eyes look up but head tips forward	Reiterate the teaching point and repeat
Waist and hips sink	Revert to the previous practice
Head moves about	Reiterate the teaching point
Failing to maintain a straight line	Assist and encourage relaxation

Body Position

Push and glide holding a float

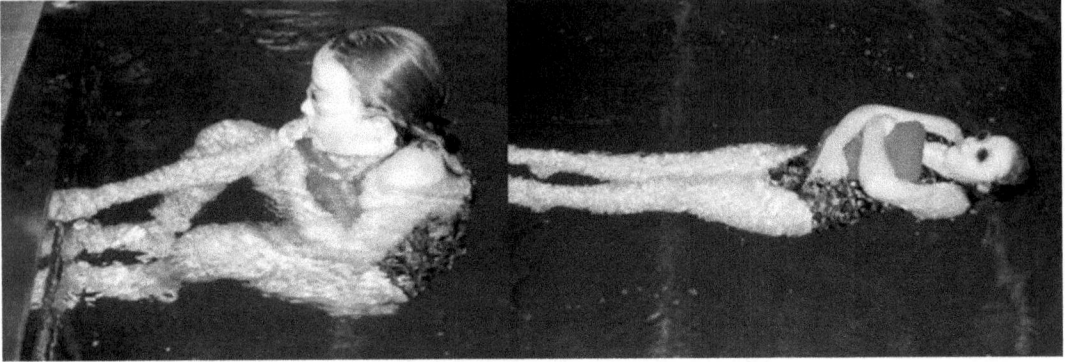

Aim: to gain confidence and move through the water in a supine position.

Holding a float gives added security to the nervous or weak swimmer whilst helping to maintain correct body position.

Teaching Points
- Relax
- Keep your head back and chin up
- Push your tummy up to the surface
- Look up to the ceiling
- Keep your head still
- Push off like a rocket

Teacher's Focus
- Overall body should be horizontal and streamlined
- Head remains still
- Eyes looking upwards
- Hips must be close to the surface
- Legs must be together

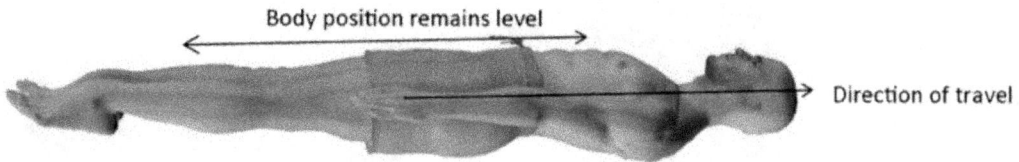

Body position remains level

Direction of travel

Float can be placed on the chest or behind the head as in the photos above.

Common Faults	Remedy
Push off is not hard enough	Reiterate the teaching point and repeat
Head raises out of the wate	Repeat the previous body position practice
Waist and hips sink	Reiterate the teaching point and repeat
Head moves about	Reiterate the teaching point
Failing to maintain a straight line	Assist and encourage relaxation

Body Position

Push and glide from the poolside without floats

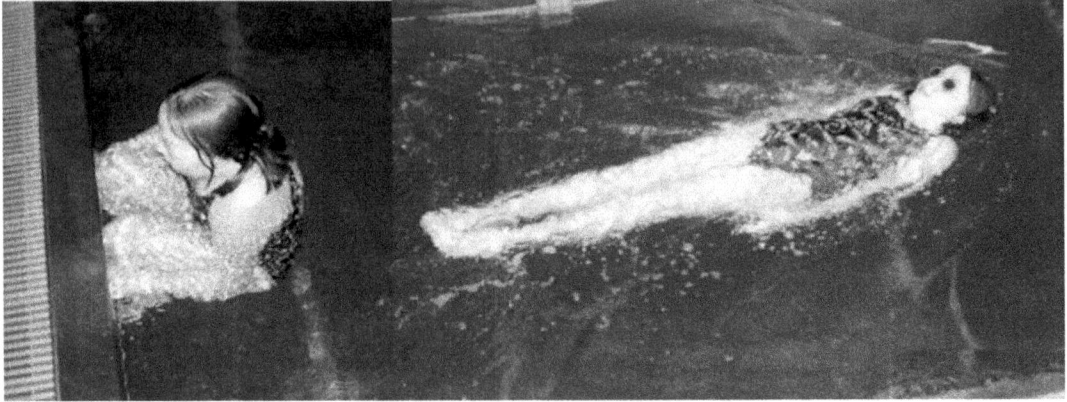

Aim: to encourage correct body position whilst moving.

The swimmer uses the momentum of a push from the poolside. Arms are held by the sides or held straight over the head in more advanced cases.

Teaching Points

- Relax
- Make your body as long as you can
- Push off like a rocket
- Push your tummy up to the surface
- Look up to the ceiling
- Glide in a long straight line

Teacher's Focus

- Overall body should be horizontal and streamlined
- Head remains still
- Eyes looking upwards and towards the feet
- Hips must be close to the surface
- Legs must be together
- Arms are held by the sides

Push and glide from the poolside without floats

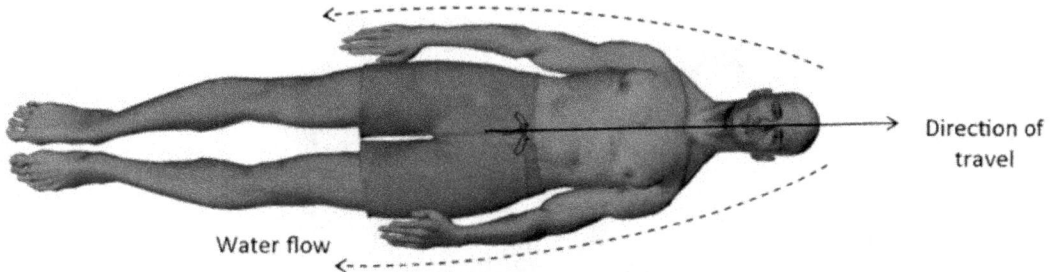

Direction of travel

Water flow

Common Faults	Remedy
Push off is not hard enough	Reiterate the teaching point and repeat
Head raises out of the water	Repeat the previous body position practice
Waist and hips sink	Reiterate the teaching point and repeat
Head moves about	Reiterate the teaching point
Failing to maintain a straight line	Reiterate the teaching point and repeat

Legs

Woggle held under the arms

Aim: to practise and develop correct leg kick action.

This exercise is ideal for the nervous beginner as an introduction to swimming on the back. The stability of the woggle encourages kicking and motion backwards with ease.

Teaching Points

- Point your toes like a ballerina
- Kick from your hips
- Kick with floppy feet
- Make a small splash with your toes

Teacher's Focus

- Kick comes from the hips
- Kick is alternating and continuous
- Kick breaks the water surface
- Hips and tummy up near the surface
- Toes are pointed and ankles relaxed
- Legs are together
- Slight knee bend

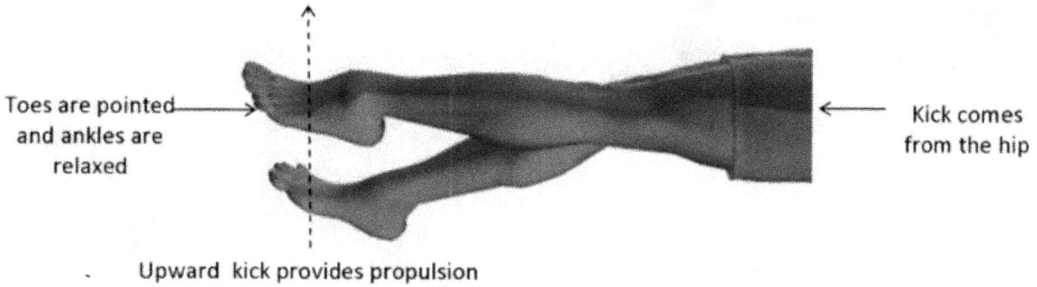

Toes are pointed
and ankles are
relaxed

Kick comes
from the hip

Upward kick provides propulsion

Common Faults	Remedy
Kick comes from the knee	Reiterate teaching point and repeat
Hips sink and legs kick too deep	Check body position and repeat
Toes are turned up	Reiterate the teaching point, demonstrate and repeat
Stiff ankles	Repeat previous leg practice
Legs are too 'stiff', not relaxed	Encourage to relax and repeat

Legs

Float held under each arm

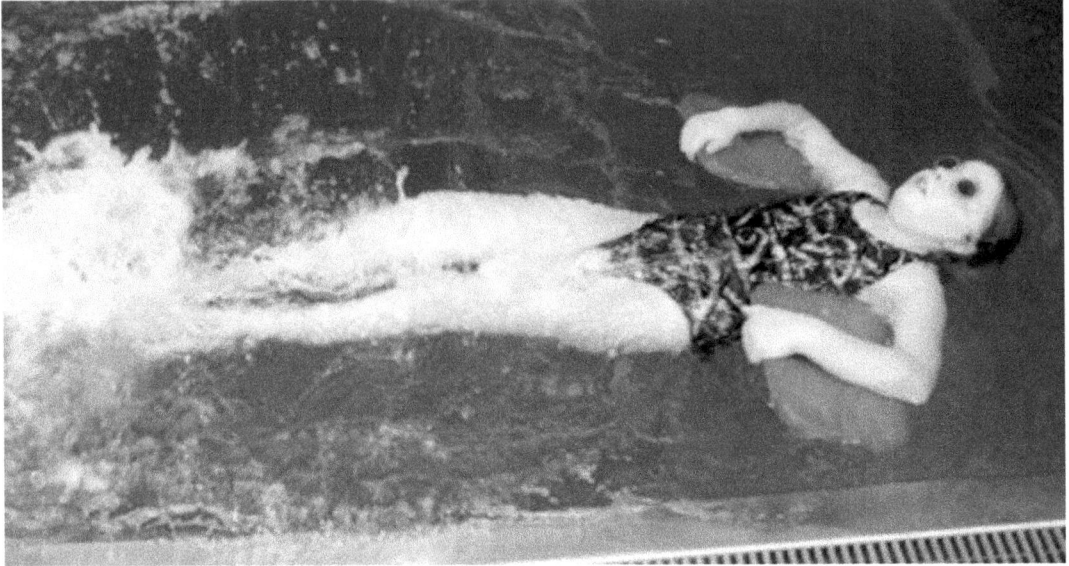

Aim: to practise and develop leg action whilst maintaining correct body position.

Two floats provide good support and encourage a relaxed body position, without creating excessive resistance through the water.

Teaching Points

- Relax and kick hard
- Point your toes like a ballerina
- Kick from your hips
- Kick with floppy feet
- Make a small splash with your toes
- Keep your legs together

Teacher's Focus

- Kick breaks the water surface
- Hips and tummy are up near the surface
- Toes are pointed and ankles relaxed
- Legs are together
- Slight knee bend
- Ankles are relaxed

Body alignment and
direction of travel

Continuous alternating upward kick
provides propulsion through the water

Common Faults	Remedy
Toes are turned up, causing a lack of motion	Reiterate teaching point and repeat
Head comes up, causing legs to sink	Repeat the earlier body position practices
Hips sink and legs kick too deep	Check the body position and repeat
Legs kick apart	Reiterate the teaching point and repeat

Legs

Float held on the chest

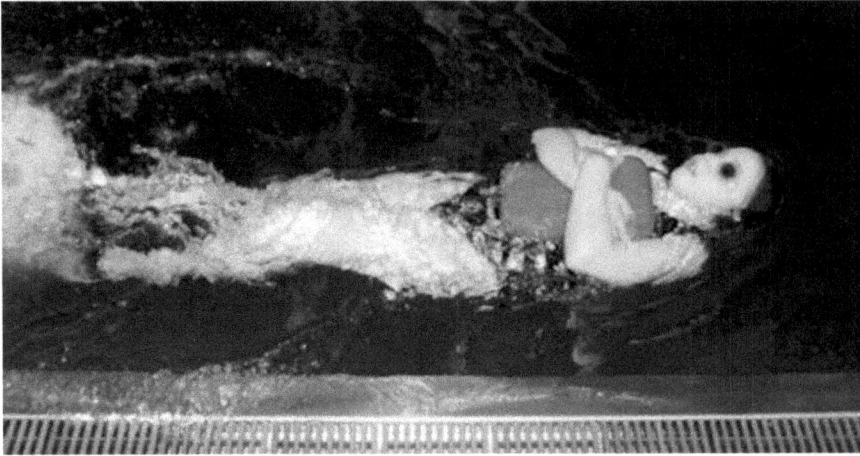

Aim: to allow the correct body position to be maintained whilst the legs kick.

This is a progression from having a float held under each arm. The swimmer is less stable but still has the security of one float held on the chest.

Teaching Points

- Point your toes like a ballerina
- Kick from your hips
- Kick with floppy feet
- Make a small splash with your toes
- Keep your legs together

Teacher's Focus

- Kick comes from the hips
- Kick is alternating and continuous
- Kick breaks the water surface
- Hips and tummy up near the surface
- Legs are together
- Ankles are relaxed and toes pointed

Ankles are relaxed and toes pointed to provide power to the upward kick ⟶

Body position remains level ⟷

Kick comes from the hip

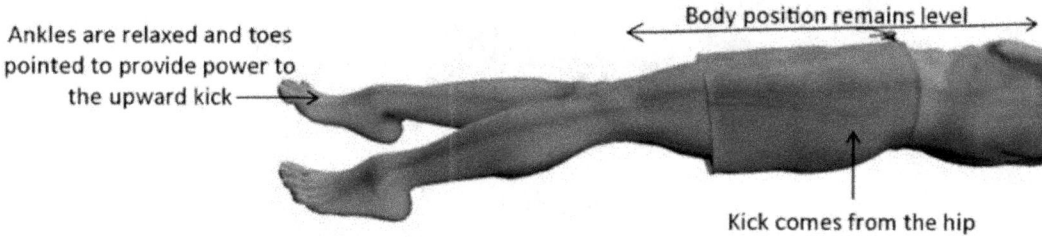

Common Faults	Remedy
Kick comes from the knee	Reiterate teaching point and repeat
Legs are kicking too deep	Repeat the previous leg practice
Toes are turned up	Repeat the earlier poolside practice
Stiff ankles	Reiterate the teaching point and repeat
Legs are too 'stiff', not relaxed	Encourage the pupil to relax and repeat

Legs

Float held behind the head

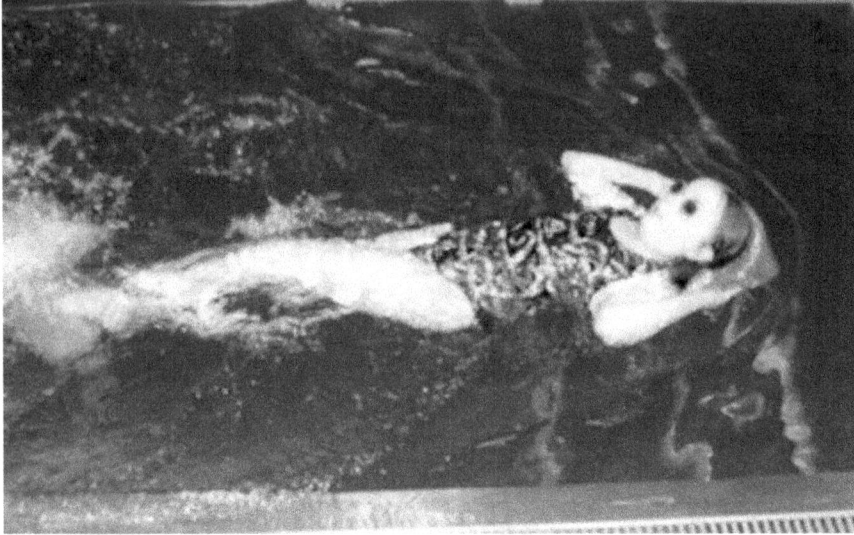

Aim: to encourage correct body position as the legs kick.

The float behind the head helps to keep the chest and hips high. A variation of the exercise with the float held on the chest, this exercise helps to develop leg strength and stamina.

Teaching Points

- Kick from your hips
- Kick with floppy feet
- Make a small splash with your toes
- Keep your legs together

Teacher's Focus

- Kick comes from the hips
- Kick breaks the water surface
- Hips and tummy up near the surface
- Toes are pointed and ankles relaxed
- Legs are together

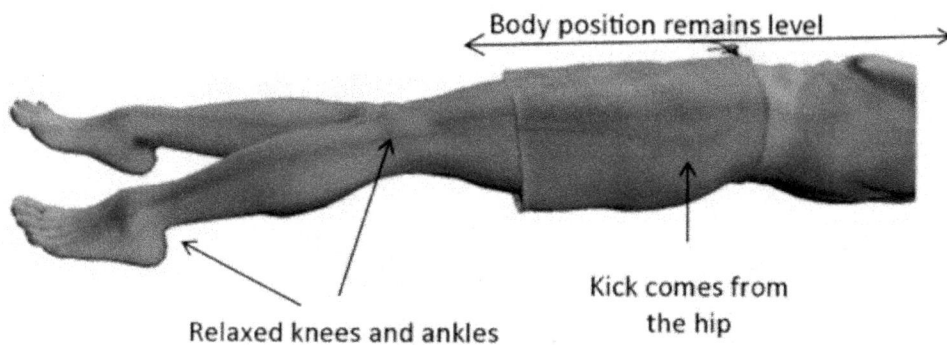

Body position remains level

Kick comes from the hip

Relaxed knees and ankles

Common Faults	Remedy
Kick comes from the knee	Repeat the earlier leg practices
Legs are kicking too deep	Check the body position and repeat
Toes are turned up	Reiterate the teaching point and repeat
Stiff ankles	Reiterate the teaching point and repeat
Legs are too 'stiff', not relaxed	Encourage the pupil to relax and repeat

Legs

Kicking with arms by the sides, hands sculling

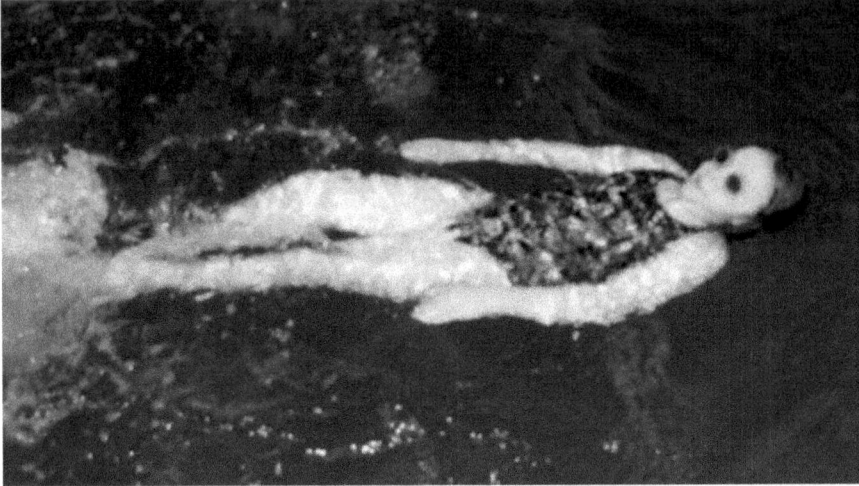

Aim: to practise kicking and maintaining correct body position on the back.

The sculling hand action provides balance and enhances confidence.

Teaching Points

- Relax
- Push your hips and chest up to the surface
- Point your toes like a ballerina
- Kick with floppy feet
- Look up to the sky

Teacher's Focus

- Kick comes from the hips
- Kick is alternating and continuous
- Kick breaks the water surface
- Hips and tummy up near the surface
- Ankles are relaxed and toes are pointed

Kicking with arms by the sides, hands sculling

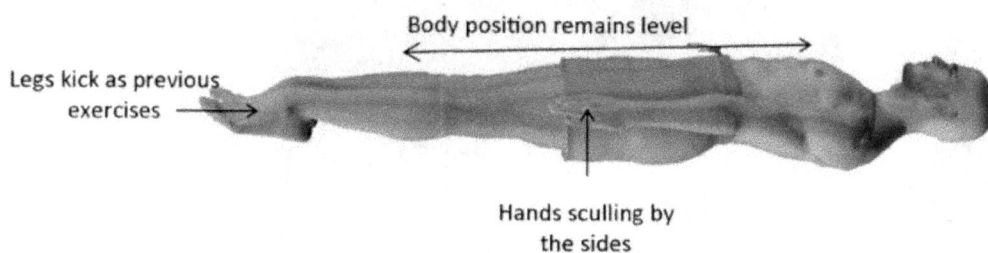

Body position remains level

Legs kick as previous exercises

Hands sculling by
the sides

Common Faults	Remedy
Kick comes from the knee	Repeat the earlier leg practices
Hips sink and legs kick too deep	Repeat the earlier body position practices
Head is too far back	Repeat the earlier body position practices
Body is not relaxed	Repeat earlier practices

Arms

Single arm pull with a float held on the chest

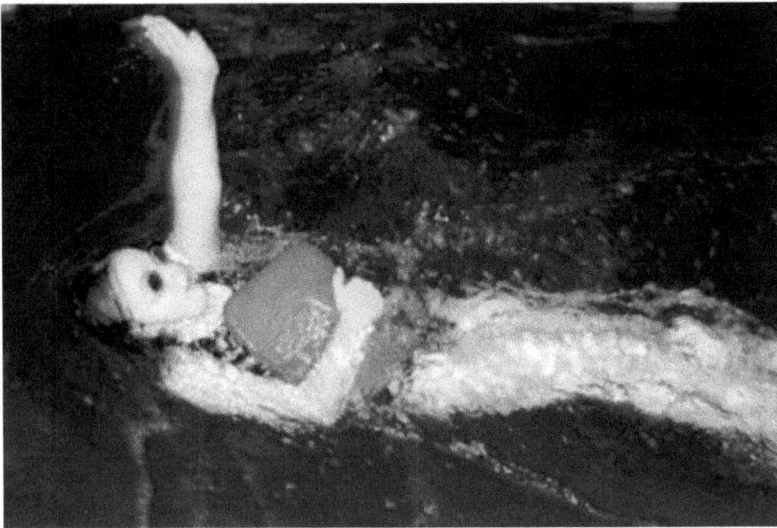

Aim: to develop correct arm action whilst kicking.

The float held on the chest provides support for the beginner and the single arm action allows easy learning without compromising the swimmer's coordination.

Teaching Points

- Arm brushes past your ear
- Pull down to your thigh
- Fingers closed together
- Little finger enters the water first

Teacher's Focus

- Arm action is continuous
- Arms stretch all the way up and brush past the ear
- Arms pull down to the thigh
- Fingers are together
- Little finger enters water first

Single arm pull with a float held on the chest

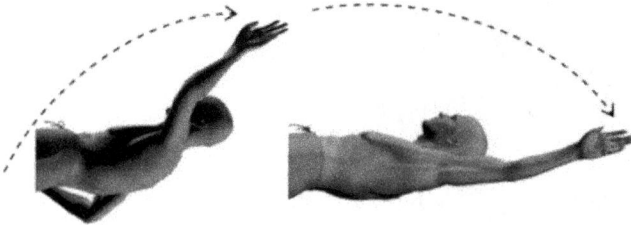

Arm exits the water and brushes past the ear, entering the water little finger first

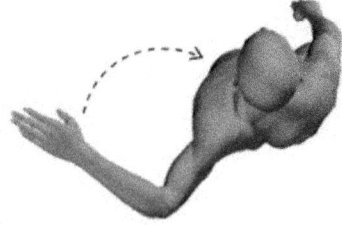

Arm is bent as it pulls through and straightens as it pulls to the thigh

Common Faults	Remedy
Arms are pulling out wide, not brushing the ear	Reiterate the teaching point and repeat
Arms are not pulling down to the side	Reiterate the teaching point and repeat
Arms pull too deep under the water	Repeat the previous arm practice
Fingers are apart	Reiterate teaching point and repeat
Thumb enters the water first	Repeat previous arm practice

Arms

Single arm pull with the opposite arm held by the side

Aim: to practise correct arm action without the aid of floats.

This single arm exercise allows focus on one arm whilst the arm held by the side encourages correct body position.

Teaching Points

- Arms brush past your ear
- Arms are continuous
- Pull down to your side
- Pull fast through the water
- Little finger enters the water first

Teacher's Focus

- Arm action is continuous
- Arms stretch all the way up and brush past the ear
- Arms pull down to the thigh
- Shoulders rock with each arm pull
- Little finger enters the water first

Single arm pull with the opposite arm held by the side

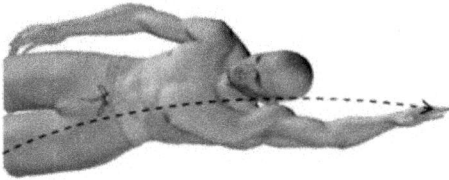

Arm rises upwards, little finger leading and arm brushing the ear

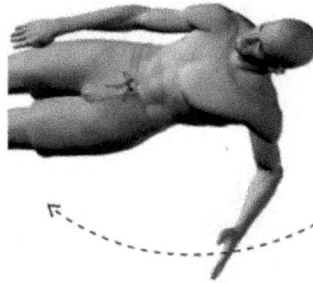

Hand pulls through the water towards the hip

Common Faults	Remedy
Arms are pulling too wide, not brushing the ear	Repeat the earlier arm practices
Arms are not pulling down to the side	Reiterate the teaching point and repeat
Arms pull too deep under the water	Repeat the earlier arm practices
Arms are bending over the head	Repeat the earlier arm practices

Breathing

Full stroke with breathing

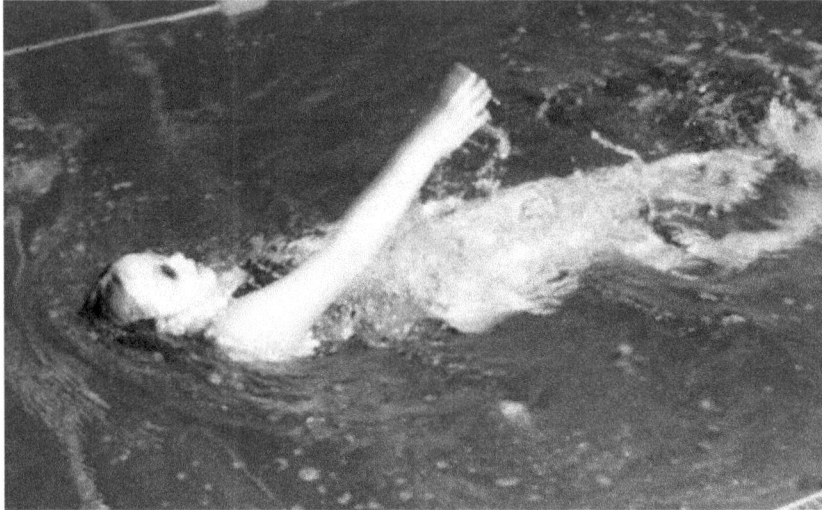

Aim: to focus on breathing in time with the stroke actions.

The swimmer should breathe in and out in regular rhythm with the arm action. This exercise can be incorporated into any of the previous arm action exercises, depending on the ability of the swimmer.

Teaching Points

- Breathe in time with your arms
- Breathe in with one arm pull and out with the other

Teacher's Focus

- Breathing should be regular and rhythmical

Breathe IN

Breathe OUT

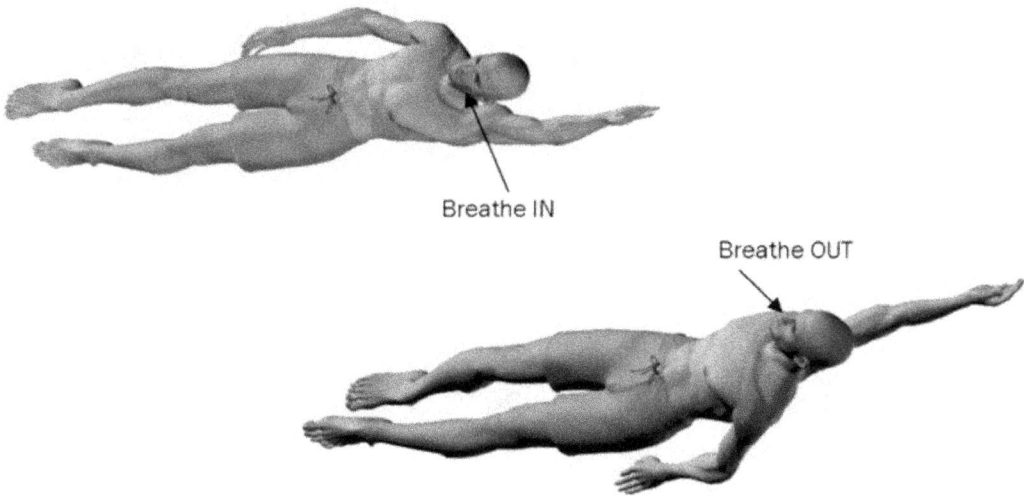

Common Faults	Remedy
Holding the breath	Repeat the static breathing practices
Breathing too rapidly	Reiterate the teaching point and repeat

Timing

Push and glide adding arms and legs

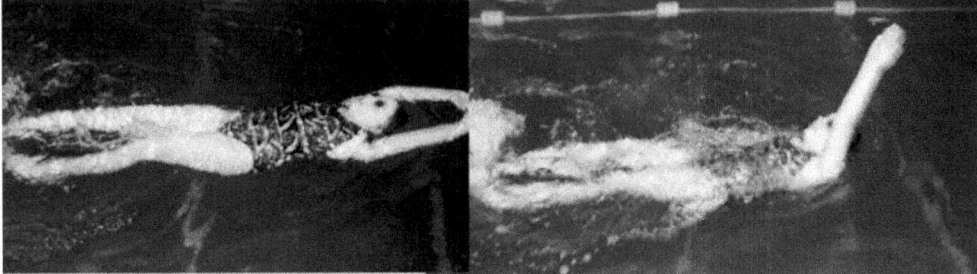

Aim: to practise and develop coordination and stroke timing.

The swimmer performs a push and glide to establish correct body position, then adds arm and leg actions.

Teaching Points

- Count in your head to 3 with each arm pull
- Kick 3 times with each arm pull
- Keep the arm pull continuous
- Keep the leg kick continuous

Teacher's Focus

- 3 leg kicks per arm pull
- Leg kick should be continuous
- Arm action should be regular

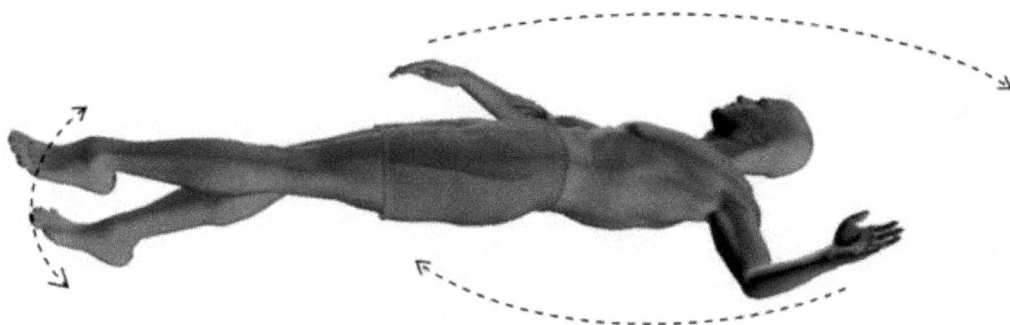

One arm exits the water as the other begins to pull and the
leg kick remains continuous

Common Faults	Remedy
One leg kick per arm pull ('one beat cycle')	Reiterate the teaching point and repeat
Continuous leg kick but not enough arm pull	Repeat the earlier arm practices
Arm pull is too irregular	Repeat the earlier arm practices
Stroke cycle is not regular and continuous	Reiterate the teaching point and repeat

Full stroke

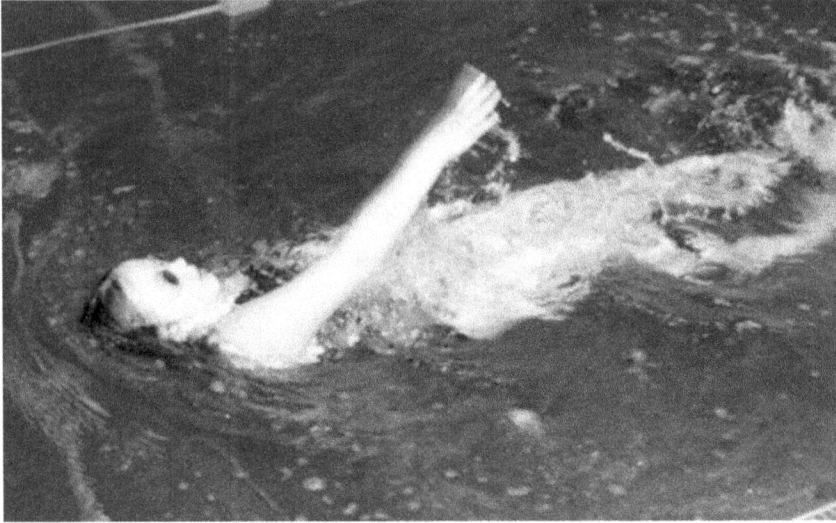

Aim: to demonstrate full stroke backstroke showing continuous and alternating arm and leg actions, with correct timing, resulting in a smooth and efficient stroke.

Teaching Points

- Kick from your hips
- Relax
- Keep your hips and tummy at the surface
- Make a small splash with your toes
- Continuous arm action
- Arms brush past your ear and pull to your side

Teacher's Focus

- Body position should be horizontal and flat
- Leg kick should be continuous and alternating
- Arm action is continuous
- Leg kick breaks the water surface
- 3 legs kicks per arm pull

Body position
remains level

Alternating leg kick
remains at the water
surface

Arm action is continuous
and alternating

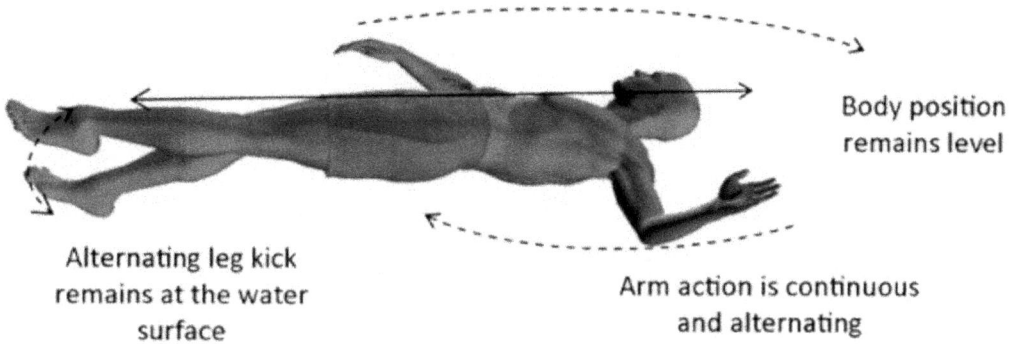

Common Faults	Remedy
Hips and abdomen sink	Repeat the earlier body position practice
Legs kick too deep or weak	Repeat the earlier leg practices
Arms pull one at a time	Repeat the earlier arm practices
Arms pull too wide or too deep	Reiterate the teaching point and repeat

Adult Lesson Plans

Lesson Plan: getting used to the water

Level: adult beginner
Previous learning: none
Lesson aim: to get used to being in the water
Equipment: buoyancy aids

Exercise/Activity	Teaching Points	Organisation	Duration
Entry: using the pool steps	take your time	all together	1 min
Warm up: walking in water of waist depth (holding the poolside if needed)	slowly at first	all together	2 mins
holding the poolside, sink down to submerge the shoulders	relax and breathe	all together	2 mins
walking into deeper water (up to shoulder depth if able)	take your time	all together	3 mins
holding the poolside, blow bubbles at the surface	breathe out slowly and gently	all together	3 mins
holding the poolside, breath holding and submerging the mouth then nose (eyes if comfortable)	relax and take your time	all together	2 mins
Moving through the water at shoulder depth, blowing bubbles	raise the mouth to inhale	all together	3 mins
Moving through water at shoulder depth, changing direction, moving backwards	relax and take your time	all together	3 mins
Contrasting Activity: holding the poolside and kicking the legs	relax your knees and ankles	waves	3 mins
Choose one exercise from this lesson to repeat	choose something you found tricky	one by one	4 mins
Exit: using the pool steps	take your time	one by one	2 min

Total time: 28 minutes

Lesson Assessment

Lesson Objective: to get used to being in the water

Below average	Average	Above average
😐	🙂	😎
Attempts to demonstrate but does not show the correct technique	Able to perform most of the technique correctly some of the time	Performs the technique correctly most of the time

Assessment	😐	🙂	😎
Walk through shallow water			
Walk into deeper water			
Exhale into the water			
Move through the water, changing direction			

Lesson Plan: floating and gliding

Level: adult beginner
Previous learning: being used to the water and face submerging
Lesson aim: to learn and gain confidence in floating and gliding
Equipment: woggles, floats and other buoyancy aids if needed

Exercise/Activity	Teaching Points	Organisation	Duration
Entry: using the pool steps	take your time	all together	1 min
Warm up: Moving through the water at shoulder depth, blowing bubbles	relax and blow	all together	2 mins
Main theme: prone star float with buoyancy aids or teacher support as needed	face in the water	one by one	3 mins
push and glide towards the side and regain standing with buoyancy aids as needed	legs together	waves	3 mins
push and glide away from the the side and regain standing with buoyancy aids as needed	stretch arms in front	waves	3 mins
supine star float with buoyancy aids or teacher support as needed	head back and relax	one by one	3 mins
push and glide on the back, away from the side	chest and hips up	waves	3 mins
mushroom float and regain standing	chin on chest	waves	3 mins
Contrasting Activity: push and glide adding kicking	slow relaxed kicks	waves	3 mins
Choose one exercise from this lesson to repeat	choose something you found tricky	one by one	4 mins
Exit: using the pool steps	take your time	one by one	1 min

Total time: 29 minutes

Lesson Assessment

Lesson Objective: to learn and gain confidence in floating and gliding		
Below average	**Average**	**Above average**
😐	🙂	😎
Attempts to demonstrate but does not show the correct technique	Able to perform most of the technique correctly some of the time	Performs the technique correctly most of the time

Assessment	😐	🙂	😎
Regain standing with buoyancy aids			
Glide towards the poolside			
Float in a supine position (with aids if needed)			
Float in a prone position (with aids if needed)			
Regain standing from a floating position			
Glide away from the poolside and regain standing			

Lesson Plan: front paddle 1

Level: adult beginner
Previous learning: kicking legs, gliding and floating
Lesson aim: to learn the basic movements needed for front paddle
Equipment: buoyancy aids as needed

Exercise/Activity	Teaching Points	Organisation	Duration
Entry: using the pool steps	take your time	all together	1 min
Warm up: Moving through the water at shoulder depth, blowing bubbles	relax and get used to the water	all together	2 mins
Main theme: push and glide using buoyancy aids if needed	push off and stretch out	waves	3 mins
holding the poolside kicking	relaxed knees and ankles	all together	2 mins
kicking using a float under each arm	floppy feet	waves	3 mins
walking through the water with arm actions	fingers together	all together	2 mins
kicking and pulling using a woggle	reach and pull	waves	3 mins
push and glide using a woggle, adding arm pulls and leg kicks	feel your way through the water	waves	3 mins
Contrasting Activity: supine star float	relax and stretch out	waves	3 mins
push and glide in a supine position, using buoyancy aids as needed	head back, chest and hips up	waves	3 mins
Exit: using the pool steps	take your time	one by one	2 min

Total time: 27 minutes

Lesson Assessment

Lesson Objective: to learn the basic movements needed for front paddle

Below average	Average	Above average
😐	🙂	😎
Attempts to demonstrate but does not show the correct technique	Able to perform most of the technique correctly some of the time	Performs the technique correctly most of the time

Assessment	😐	🙂	😎
Leg kick is alternating			
Leg kick provides some propulsion			
Uses arms in a pulling action			
Uses arms and legs simultaneously			

Lesson Plan: front paddle 2

Level: adult beginner
Previous learning: basic alternating front kicking and pulling action
Lesson aim: to learn and develop an independent front paddle
Equipment: woggles and buoyancy aids as needed

Exercise/Activity	Teaching Points	Organisation	Duration
Entry: swivel entry or using the pool steps	take your time	all together	1 min
Warm up: kicking and pulling using a woggle	relax, kick and pull	all together	2 mins
Main theme: kicking using a float under each arm	kick with relaxed ankles	waves	3 mins
push and glide from the poolside	relax and stretch	waves	3 mins
push and glide adding leg kicks	kick from the hips	waves	3 mins
front paddle using a woggle, adding breathing	blow gently across the water	waves	3 mins
push and glide, exhaling through the glide, regain standing	relax and blow	waves	3 mins
push and glide, adding arm pulls and leg kicks, regain standing	feel your way through the water	waves	3 mins
Contrasting Activity: supine star float and regain standing	head back, chest and hips up	waves	3 mins
leg kicks in a supine position with a woggle	deep breath and stretch down	one by one	3 mins
Exit: using the pool steps	take your time	one by one	2 min

Total time: 29 minutes

Lesson Assessment

Lesson Objective: to learn and develop an independent front paddle		
Below average 🙂	**Average** 🙂	**Above average** 😎
Attempts to demonstrate but does not show the correct technique	Able to perform most of the technique correctly some of the time	Performs the technique correctly most of the time

Assessment	😐	🙂	😎
Leg kick is alternating and continuous			
Leg kick provides some propulsion			
Arm action is alternating			
Arm action provides propulsion			
Demonstrates a breathing technique			

Lesson Plan: back paddle 1

Level: adult beginner
Previous learning: basic alternating kicking and supine floating
Lesson aim: to learn a basic back paddle
Equipment: buoyancy aids as needed

Exercise/Activity	Teaching Points	Organisation	Duration
Entry: using the pool steps	take your time	all together	1 min
Warm up: 2 widths moving through the water (walking or swimming with aids as needed)	relax and feel the water	all together	2 mins
Main theme: push and glide with a woggle	look up to the sky	waves	3 mins
supine kicking with a woggle	pointed toes	waves	3 mins
walking backwards through the water using arm action	stroke the dog	waves	3 mins
supine kicking with a woggle, adding arm pulls, regain standing	kick from the hips	waves	3 mins
push and glide with woggle, adding arm pulls, leg kicks and regain standing	relax and breathe	waves	3 mins
supine floating, adding leg kicks and gentle arm movements - with teacher assistance as needed	relaxed gentle movements	one by one	4 mins
Contrasting Activity: supine star float, roll onto the front and regain standing	knees to your chest when standing	waves	2 mins
prone push and glide to submerge (reach the pool floor if possible)	deep breath and stretch downwards	waves	3 mins
Exit: using the pool steps	take your time	one by one	1 min

Total time: 28 minutes

Lesson Assessment

Lesson Objective: to learn a basic back paddle

Below average	Average	Above average
😐	🙂	😎
Attempts to demonstrate but does not show the correct technique	Able to perform most of the technique correctly some of the time	Performs the technique correctly most of the time

Assessment	😐	🙂	😎
Leg kick is alternating			
Kicks are from the hips			
Head is back, eyes facing upwards			
Arm action is relaxed			

Lesson Plan: back paddle 2

Level: adult beginner
Previous learning: basic kicking and arm action on the back with aids
Lesson aim: to develop an independent back paddle
Equipment: buoyancy aids and sinkers

Exercise/Activity	Teaching Points	Organisation	Duration
Entry: swivel entry or using the pool steps	take your time	all together	1 min
Warm up: 2 widths with buoyancy aids if needed	relax and take your time	all together	2 mins
Main theme: supine push and glide	push your chest up	one by one	3 mins
kicking using a float under each arm	flick your toes up	waves	3 mins
supine kicking with a woggle adding arm pulls	polish the water	waves	3 mins
supine push and glide, adding arm pulls and leg kicks, regaining standing	head back, chest up	waves	3 mins
push and glide into back paddle for a short distance, regaining standing	knees to chest when standing	waves	3 mins
push and glide into back paddle, increasing distance of the swim	continuous arms and legs	waves	3 mins
Contrasting Activity: supine push and glide, roll onto the front and continue swimming prone	smooth, slow movements	waves	3 mins
submerge to collect an object	eyes open	one by one	3 mins
Exit: using the pool steps	take your time	one by one	1 min

Total time: 28 minutes

Lesson Assessment

Lesson Objective: to develop an independent back paddle		
Below average	**Average**	**Above average**
😐	🙂	😎
Attempts to demonstrate but does not show the correct technique	Able to perform most of the technique correctly some of the time	Performs the technique correctly most of the time

Assessment	😐	🙂	😎
Leg kick is alternating and continuous			
Kicks with relaxed ankles and pointed toes			
Head is back			
Chest and hips are up			
Arm action is relaxed with fingers together			
Able to swim a predetermined distance*			

*distance should be set on a pupil by pupil basis and the teacher should use their professional judgement to set this as means of encouragement.

Lesson Plan: basic breaststroke 1

Level: adult beginner
Previous learning: front paddle and floating
Lesson aim: to learn the basics of breaststroke
Equipment: floats and woggles

Exercise/Activity	Teaching Points	Organisation	Duration
Entry: swivel or steps entry	enter slowly	all together	1 min
Warm up: 2 widths any stroke with buoyancy aids if needed	take your time	all together	3 mins
Main Theme: sitting on the poolside demonstrating kicking action	kick in a circular path	all together	2 mins
supine kicking with woggle under arms	turn out your feet	waves	3 mins
Kicking with a float under each arm	kick and glide	waves	3 mins
arm pulls, walking through shallow water	keep hands underwater	waves	4 mins
arm pulls with breathing, woggle under the arms	blow your hands forwards	waves	3 mins
full stroke, with bouyancy aids if needed	pull *then* kick	waves	3 mins
Contrasting Activity: supine star float	stretch out and relax	all together	2 mins
back paddle for a pre determined distance	relax and kick	waves	3 mins
Exit: using the pool steps or over the poolside	take your time	one by one	1 min

Total time: 28 minutes

Lesson Assessment

Lesson Objective: to learn the basics of breaststroke

Below average	Average	Above average
😐	🙂	😎
Attempts to demonstrate but does not show the correct technique	Able to perform most of the technique correctly some of the time	Performs the technique correctly most of the time

Assessment	😐	🙂	😎
Arms pull in a circular path			
Legs kick in a circular path			
Feet attempt to turn outwards			
Exhalation takes place underwater			
Arm pull and leg kick sequence is continuous			

Lesson Plan: basic breaststroke 2

Level: adult beginner
Previous learning: basic breaststroke technique
Lesson aim: to progress and develop basic breaststroke
Equipment: floats

Exercise/Activity	Teaching Points	Organisation	Duration
Entry: swivel or sitting dive entry	enter slowly	waves	1 min
Warm up: 2 widths any stroke	take your time	all together	3 mins
Main Theme: 2 widths full stroke breaststroke with buoyancy aids if needed	pull in a circle, kick in a circle	waves	2 mins
push and glide from the poolside	hands and feet together	one by one	3 mins
kicking with a float under each arm	knees together and kick around	waves	3 mins
kicking with a single float held in front, adding a glide after each kick	kick hard and then glide	waves	3 mins
kicking with a float, adding breathing	kick and blow out	waves	3 mins
full stroke without buoyancy aids	kick your hands into a glide	waves	3 mins
Contrasting Activity: swim and change direction without touching the pool floor	relax and take your time	waves	3 mins
Choose one exercise from this lesson to repeat	choose something you found tricky	waves	3 mins
Exit: using the pool steps or over the poolside	take your time	one by one	1 min

Total time: 28 minutes

Lesson Assessment

Lesson Objective: to progress and develop basic breaststroke		
Below average	**Average**	**Above average**
😐	🙂	😎
Attempts to demonstrate but does not show the correct technique	Able to perform most of the technique correctly some of the time	Performs the technique correctly most of the time

Assessment	😐	🙂	😎
Arms pull in a small circle			
Legs kick in a circular path with knees close together			
Feet attempt to turn outwards			
A glide is attempted after each stroke			
Arms pull and legs kick in an alternating sequence.			

Lesson Plan: confidence building 1

Level: adult beginner
Previous learning: moving around in the water and partial submersion
Lesson aim: to increase water confidence
Equipment: buoyancy aids as needed

Exercise/Activity	Teaching Points	Organisation	Duration
Entry: swivel entry or using the pool steps	take your time	all together	1 min
Warm up: holding the poolside and kicking the legs	splash your feet	all together	2 mins
holding the poolside, exhaling at the surface - repeat*	blow gently	all together	2 mins
breath holding and submerging the mouth and nose - repeat	deep breath and hold it all in	all together	3 mins
holding the poolside, breath holding and completely submerge - repeat	slowly down and slowly up	all together	3 mins
breath holding and completely submerge without holding the poolside - repeat	relax and take your time	all together	3 mins
push and glide towards the poolside in a prone position and regain standing	stretch out and relax	waves	4 mins
prone star float and regain standing position	slow, gradual movements	waves	3 mins
Contrasting Activity: submerging to collect an object (teacher assisted by holding the object)	eyes open	one by one	3 mins
Choose one exercise from this lesson to repeat choose something you found tricky	choose something you found tricky	one by one	3 mins
Exit: using the pool steps	take your time	one by one	1 min

Total time: 28 minutes

*repetition of submersion exercises is key to enhancing confidence. Professional judgement should be used to determine the number of repetitions and the time to move on to another exercise.

Lesson Assessment

Lesson Objective: to increase water confidence		
Below average	**Average**	**Above average**
😐	🙂	😎
Attempts to demonstrate but does not show the correct technique	Able to perform most of the technique correctly some of the time	Performs the technique correctly most of the time

Assessment	😐	🙂	😎
Exhale at the water surface			
Submerges the mouth and nose			
Submerges completely			
Push and glide and regain standing			
Regains standing from prone			

Lesson Plan: confidence building 2

Level: adult beginner
Previous learning: gliding, submersion and exhaling
Lesson aim: to develop and enhance water confidence
Equipment: buoyancy aids if needed

Exercise/Activity	Teaching Points	Organisation	Duration
Entry: using the pool steps	take your time	all together	1 min
Warm up: push and glide towards the poolside in a prone position and regain standing	slowly regain a standing position	all together	3 mins
holding the poolside, breath holding and completely submerge - repeat*	slowly down and slowly up	all together	2 mins
breath holding and completely submerge without holding the poolside - repeat	relax and take your time	waves	2 mins
push and glide from the poolside exhaling through the glide - regain standing	glide and gently blow out	waves	3 mins
prone star float and regain standing position - repeat	slow, gradual movements	waves	3 mins
supine push and glide and regain standing - repeat	knees to chest	waves	3 mins
push and glide from the poolside and return without touching the pool floor	relaxed, smooth movements	waves	3 mins
Contrasting Activity: introduce treading water (shoulder depth)	relax and keep your head up	waves	3 mins
Choose one exercise from this lesson to repeat choose something you found tricky	choose something you found tricky	one by one	3 mins
Exit: using the pool steps	take your time	one by one	1 min

Total time: 27 minutes

*repetition of certain exercises are key to enhancing confidence. Professional judgement should be used to determine the number of repetitions and the time to move on to another exercise.

Lesson Assessment

Lesson Objective: to develop and enhance water confidence		
Below average	**Average**	**Above average**
😐	🙂	😎
Attempts to demonstrate but does not show the correct technique	Able to perform most of the technique correctly some of the time	Performs the technique correctly most of the time

Assessment	😐	🙂	😎
Breath holds and submerges completely			
Regains a standing position from prone			
Regains a standing position from supine			
Confidently push and glide			
Returns to the poolside without touching the pool floor			

Lesson Plan: swimming in deep water

Level: adult beginner
Previous learning: basic front paddle, submerging and floating
Lesson aim: to gain confidence in swimming out of depth
Equipment: buoyancy aids if needed

Exercise/Activity	Teaching Points	Organisation	Duration
Entry: swivel entry or using the pool steps	take your time	all together	1 min
Warm up: swim 2 widths any stroke (within depth)	relaxed kicking	all together	2 mins
Main theme: prone push and glide and return to the start without touching the pool floor	toes up and kick	waves	3 mins
supine push and glide and return to the start without touching the pool floor	face down on the way back	waves	3 mins
swim away from poolside, change direction and return without touching pool floor	face down and kick continuously	waves	3 mins
DEEP WATER: push away from the poolside and return swimming front paddle	jump away from the side	waves	3 mins
DEEP WATER: swim a predetermined distance from deep to shallow water	relax and take your time	waves	3 mins
DEEP WATER: swim a predetermined distance from shallow to deep water	continuous kicking and pulling	waves	3 mins
Contrasting Activity: introduce treading water (shoulder depth)	relax and keep your head up	waves	3 mins
Choose one exercise from this lesson to repeat choose something you found tricky	choose something you found tricky	one by one	3 mins
Exit: using the pool steps	take your time	one by one	1 min

Total time: 28 minutes

Lesson Assessment

Lesson Objective: to gain confidence in swimming out of depth

Below average	Average	Above average
😐	🙂	😎
Attempts to demonstrate but does not show the correct technique	Able to perform most of the technique correctly some of the time	Performs the technique correctly most of the time

Assessment	😐	🙂	😎
Return to the poolside from a push and glide			
Return to the poolside from a supine position			
Confidently enters deep water			
Swim from deep water to shallow			
Swim from shallow water to deep			

Lesson Plan: full stroke front crawl 1

Level: adult or child beginner
Previous learning: basic front paddle
Lesson aim: to learn each part of basic front crawl and experience the whole stroke
Equipment: floats, buoyancy aids and hoop

Exercise/Activity	Teaching Points	Organisation	Duration
Entry: swivel or steps entry	enter slowly	all together	1 min
Warm up: 2 widths any stroke with buoyancy aids if needed	take your time	all together	3 mins
Main Theme: push and glide, holding a float if needed	stretch out and glide	one by one	2 mins
kicking whilst holding a float under each arm	kick with floppy feet	all together	2 mins
single arm pull with a float held under one arm. repeat with opposite arm.	elbow leads out first	waves	4 mins
holding a float with a diagonal grip. repeat with head turning to the opposite side.	turn head to the bent elbow	waves	4 mins
alternate arm pulls holding float out in front	Count '1,2,3' each pull	waves	3 mins
full stroke front crawl	continuous arm pulls and leg kicks	waves	3 mins
Contrasting Activity: jumping entry and swim through a hoop	jump away from the side	2 or 3 at a time	3 mins
sitting dive through a hoop at the surface	head tucked down	2 or 3 at a time	3 mins
Exit: using the pool steps or over the poolside	take your time	one by one	1 min

Total time: 29 minutes

Lesson Assessment

Lesson Objective: to learn each part of basic front crawl and experience the whole stroke

Below average	Average	Above average
😐	🙂	😎
Attempts to demonstrate but does not show the correct technique	Able to perform most of the technique correctly some of the time	Performs the technique correctly most of the time

Assessment	😐	🙂	😎
Face in and out of the water as they move across the pool			
Kick leg is alternating			
Arms recover over the water surface			
Able to breathe without pausing			
Leg kicks and arm pulls are continuous			

Lesson Plan: full stroke front crawl 2

Level: adult or child intermediate
Previous learning: basic front crawl technique
Lesson aim: to progress and develop the whole stroke to an intermediate level
Equipment: floats, pull buoys, sinkers and hoop

Exercise/Activity	Teaching Points	Organisation	Duration
Entry: swivel or sitting dive entry	enter slowly	waves	1 min
Warm up: 2 widths any stroke	take your time	all together	3 mins
Main Theme: push and glide from the side	hands and feet together	one by one	2 mins
kicking whilst holding a float in both hands	kick with long legs	waves	3 mins
arms only using a pull buoy between the legs	pull and stretch	waves	3 mins
holding a float with a diagonal grip	breathe out slowly	waves	3 mins
push and glide, add arms pulls and leg kicks	continuous arm and legs	waves	3 mins
full stroke front crawl	steady and relaxed	waves	3 mins
Contrasting Activity: head first surface dives, collecting sinkers placed apart	deep breath and dig down	one by one	3 mins
dolphin kick through a hoop at the surface	swim like a mermaid	one by one	3 mins
Exit: using the pool steps or over the poolside	take your time	one by one	1 min

Total time: 28 minutes

Lesson Assessment

Lesson Objective: to progress and develop the whole stroke to an intermediate level

Below average	Average	Above average
😐	🙂	😎
Attempts to demonstrate but does not show the correct technique	Able to perform most of the technique correctly some of the time	Performs the technique correctly most of the time

Assessment	😐	🙂	😎
Body position is horizontal			
Kick legs from the hips			
Kicks with toes pointed			
Finger and thumb enter the water first			
Head rolls to the side to breathe			
Leg kicks and arm pulls are alternating and continuous			

Lesson Plan: full stroke breaststroke 1

Level: adult or child beginner
Previous learning: Child - basic front paddle Adult - none
Lesson aim: to learn the basics of breaststroke and experience the whole stroke
Equipment: floats, woggle, buoyancy aids if needed and hoop

Exercise/Activity	Teaching Points	Organisation	Duration
Entry: swivel or steps entry	enter slowly	all together	1 min
Warm up: 2 widths any stroke with buoyancy aids if needed	take your time	all together	3 mins
Main Theme: full stroke, slowly with a woggle under the arms	pull in a circle, kick in a circle	all together	2 mins
push and glide, holding floats if needed	stretch out and relax	waves	3 mins
supine kicking with woggle under arms	turn out your feet	waves	3 mins
arm pulls, walking through shallow water	keep hands underwater	waves	4 mins
arm pulls with breathing, woggle under the arms	blow your hands forwards	waves	3 mins
full stroke, with bouyancy aids if needed	pull *then* kick	waves	3 mins
Contrasting Activity: supine star float	stretch out and relax	2 or 3 at a time	3 mins
sitting dive through a hoop at the surface	head tucked down	2 or 3 at a time	3 mins
Exit: using the pool steps or over the poolside	take your time	one by one	1 min

Total time: 29 minutes

Lesson Assessment

Lesson Objective: to learn each part of basic breaststroke and experience the whole stroke

Below average	Average	Above average
😐	🙂	😎
Attempts to demonstrate but does not show the correct technique	Able to perform most of the technique correctly some of the time	Performs the technique correctly most of the time

Assessment	😐	🙂	😎
Arms pull in a circular path			
Legs kick in a circular path			
Feet attempt to turn outwards			
Exhalation takes place underwater			
Arm pull and leg kick sequence is continuous			

Lesson Plan: full stroke breaststroke 2

Level: adult or child intermediate
Previous learning: basic breaststroke technique
Lesson aim: to progress and develop the whole stroke to an intermediate level
Equipment: floats, sinkers and hoop

Exercise/Activity	Teaching Points	Organisation	Duration
Entry: swivel or sitting dive entry	enter slowly	waves	1 min
Warm up: 2 widths any stroke	take your time	all together	3 mins
Main Theme: 2 widths full stroke breaststroke with buoyancy aids if needed	pull in a circle, kick in a circle	waves	2 mins
push and glide from the poolside	hands and feet together	one by one	3 mins
kicking with a float under each arm	knees together and kick around	waves	3 mins
push and glide adding arm pulls	pull in small circles	waves	3 mins
kicking with a float, adding breathing	kick and blow out	waves	3 mins
full stroke without buoyancy aids	kick your hands forwards	waves	3 mins
Contrasting Activity: head first surface dives, collecting sinkers placed apart	deep breath and dig down	one by one	3 mins
dolphin kick through a hoop at the surface	swim like a mermaid	one by one	3 mins
Exit: using the pool steps or over the poolside	take your time	one by one	1 min

Total time: 28 minutes

Lesson Assessment

Lesson Objective: to progress and develop the whole stroke to an intermediate level		
Below average	**Average**	**Above average**
😐	🙂	😎
Attempts to demonstrate but does not show the correct technique	Able to perform most of the technique correctly some of the time	Performs the technique correctly most of the time

Assessment	😐	🙂	😎
Arms pull in a small circle			
Legs kick in a circular path with knees close together			
Feet attempt to turn outwards			
Exhalation takes place as the legs kick around and back			
Arms pull and legs kick in an alternating sequence.			

Lesson Plan: full stroke backstroke 1

Level: adult or child beginner
Previous learning: basic alternating kicking and supine floating
Lesson aim: to learn the basics of backstroke and experience the whole stroke
Equipment: floats, woggle, buoyancy aids if needed and hoop

Exercise/Activity	Teaching Points	Organisation	Duration
Entry: swivel or steps entry	enter slowly	all together	1 min
Warm up: 2 widths any stroke with buoyancy aids if needed	take your time	all together	3 mins
Main Theme: kicking supine with a woggle under the arms	relax and kick	all together	2 mins
supine push and glide, holding floats if needed	hips up and stretch	waves	3 mins
supine kicking with a float held on the chest	kick with pointed toes	waves	3 mins
single arm pulls with a float held on the chest	arm stretches up and back	waves	3 mins
single arm pulls using the opposite arm with a float held on the chest	fingers together	waves	3 mins
2 widths full stroke backstroke	kick and pull continuously	waves	3 mins
Contrasting Activity: prone star float	deep breath and relax	2 or 3 at a time	3 mins
sitting dive through a hoop at the surface	head tucked down	2 or 3 at a time	3 mins
Exit: using the pool steps or over the poolside	take your time	one by one	1 min

Total time: 28 minutes

Lesson Assessment

Lesson Objective: to learn the basics of backstroke and experience the whole stroke

Below average	Average	Above average
😐	🙂	😎
Attempts to demonstrate but does not show the correct technique	Able to perform most of the technique correctly some of the time	Performs the technique correctly most of the time

Assessment	😐	🙂	😎
Head is facing upwards			
Hips are at or near the surface			
Legs kick alternately			
Toes are pointed			
Arm pulls are continuous			

Lesson Plan: full stroke backstroke 2

Level: adult or child intermediate
Previous learning: basic backstroke technique
Lesson aim: to progress and develop the whole stroke to an intermediate level
Equipment: floats, pull buoy, sinkers and hoop

Exercise/Activity	Teaching Points	Organisation	Duration
Entry: swivel or sitting dive entry	enter slowly	waves	1 min
Warm up: 2 widths any stroke	take your time	all together	3 mins
Main Theme: 2 widths full stroke backstroke with buoyancy aids if needed	pull and kick continuously	waves	2 mins
supine push and glide from the poolside	head back, looking upwards	one by one	3 mins
supine kicking with a float behind the head	kick with floppy feet	waves	3 mins
arm pulls with a pull buoy	pull through to your thighs	waves	3 mins
arm pulls with a pull buoy, adding breathing	pull and blow	waves	3 mins
full stroke backstroke without buoyancy aids	kick your hands forwards	waves	3 mins
Contrasting Activity: head first surface dives, collecting sinkers placed apart	deep breath and dig down	one by one	3 mins
dolphin kick through a hoop at the surface	swim like a mermaid	one by one	3 mins
Exit: using the pool steps or over the poolside	take your time	one by one	1 min

Total time: 28 minutes

Lesson Assessment

Lesson Objective: to progress and develop the whole stroke to an intermediate level		
Below average	**Average**	**Above average**
😐	🙂	😎
Attempts to demonstrate but does not show the correct technique	**Able to perform most of the technique correctly some of the time**	**Performs the technique correctly most of the time**

Assessment	😐	🙂	😎
Head is facing upwards with ears in the water			
Hips and tummy are at water surface			
Legs kick alternately with relaxed ankles			
Toes are pointed			
Arms pull through to the thighs			

The Perfect Companions To This Book

101 Swimming Lesson Plans for Swimming Teachers.

Ready-made lesson plans that take the hard work out of planning.

Every lesson plan from first entering the water to swimming advanced butterfly.

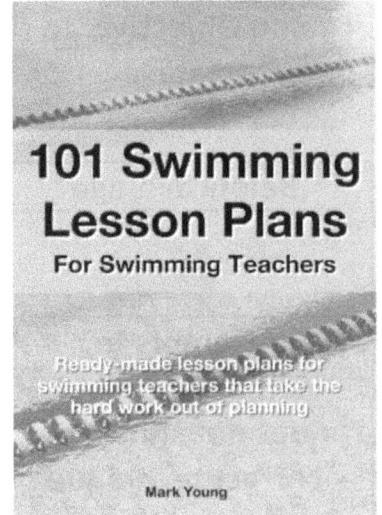

How To Be A Swimming Teacher

The Definitive Guide To Teaching Outstanding Swimming Lessons.

Discover:
- *teaching qualities*
- *best practices*
- *82 basic drills*

Become the best swimming teacher you can be!

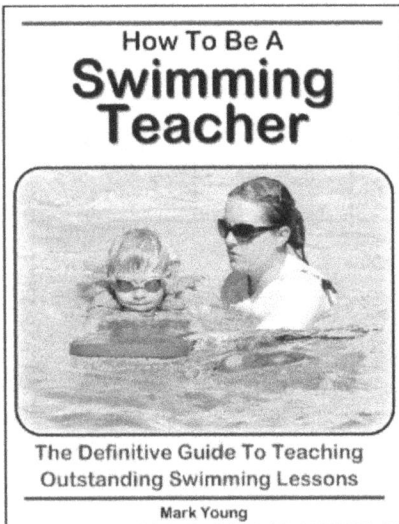

Available as an ebook to download from **Swim-Teach.com** or in print from most online retailers.

**An electronic version of this book is available
from Swim-Teach.com**

"Now that you have finished my book, would you please consider writing a review? Reviews are the best way readers discover great new books. I would truly appreciate it."

Mark Young

For more information about teaching swimming, learning to swim and improving swimming technique visit **Swim Teach**.

Swim Teach
Teaching · Learning · Achieving · *Professional Swimming Help Online*

www.swim-teach.com